action&
character
an introduction to moral philosophy
an introduction to moral philosophy

ALEXANDER R. EODICE

Iona College

Kendall Hunt
publishing company

www.kendallhunt.com
Send all inquiries to:
4050 Westmark Drive
Dubuque, IA 52004-1840

Copyright © 2016 by Kendall Hunt Publishing Company

ISBN 978-1-4652-7505-9

Printed in the United States of America

In memory of Ralph A. Eodice—my father, my friend, my moral hero

Contents

Acknowledgments

This is a small introductory book, but there are some people who deserve a large measure of my gratitude. Many thanks to the folks at Kendall Hunt Publishing Company, especially Melissa Lavenz, who sold me on the idea of writing an introductory text, and Beth Trowbridge, whose guidance on the production end has been invaluable, and thanks to both for their patience in waiting for my submissions. Thanks also to Karen Fleckenstein for her editorial assistance and skillful design work.

I am grateful to my colleagues in the philosophy department at Iona College; I am inspired always by their professionalism, dedication, and collegiality. I owe a special debt of gratitude to the many students who have endured my ramblings over the years; they have taught me more than they may ever realize. Special thanks to Michael Jordan for reading part of this manuscript and to Dom Balestra, my teacher and critic, a fellow philosopher, and, most important, my life-long friend.

My deepest gratitude goes to family. My mother, Anne, continues to provide sustenance for the body in the way of wonderful meals and for the soul with her wise and loving guidance. My grown daughters, Sarah and Annie, still bring me the greatest joy and always remind me what makes life worthwhile. Most especially, I am grateful to my wife, Liz, whose love, support, and good humor get me through every day and whose character is the finest of any person I know.

Thinking About Morality

This book is an introduction to that branch of philosophy called moral philosophy or ethics (those terms are used interchangeably here); that is, it is a guide to understanding fundamental concepts that are employed when we think about what it means to be moral. As self-reflective creatures, we wonder, for instance, about right and wrong actions, about good and bad character, about what we should value and what goals we should pursue. Such issues constitute the core ideas that define the moral life and characterize our ordinary moral experience. Morality is not simply about doing things which have, in some abstract sense, been determined to be right or about just doing what is expected of us; it is the result of thoughtful consideration about how we ought to act in the world and about what kind of persons we should strive to be. Thinking about morality is a complex undertaking. In this work I hope to make that complexity a little less daunting by linking philosophical theories with common conceptions of moral experience.

Morality seems, quite naturally, to pervade many salient aspects of human life. As children, if we are fortunate enough to be guided by the example of good parents or guardians, we are taught, for instance, to share appropriately, to play honestly and fairly, to respect the feelings and needs of others. Over time, such behaviors may become second nature to us and we may come to choose to act in ways consistent with that early guidance. As we mature as individual persons, we come to hold various positions and make judgments about large-scale moral issues—war, abortion, global hunger and world poverty, capital punishment, the environment, human sexuality, etc. But morality is not just a compartment of human life, or not simply a specified set of principles or ideas that we consult when thinking about such large issues. In fact, the deepest, most challenging moral concerns are much closer to home. Should we tell a lie if it keeps us out of trouble? Should we breech the confidence of a friend when we know that doing so will help that person? What, if any, obligations do children owe to their aging parents? What efforts should we put into work and how do we balance this with other elements of life—family obligations, community concerns, and personal leisure? What special obligations might friendship require of us? Putting the matter this way sets into relief the pervasive character of morality in ordinary, everyday human experience.

Of course, not everything we do has moral implications. Consider simple preferences: You prefer to wear wingtips, I like loafers; you order breakfast food in a diner at dinnertime, while I prefer to eat a hefty order of beef stew; you prefer Brahams to Bach or the Beastie Boys to the Beatles, and my preferences may run in exactly the opposite direction; you like cranberry juice, I like orange juice. We can multiply such examples endlessly, but the point is the same in each case. These differences in preference do not (or at least should not) occasion our moral judgments about others. But there is a larger point to be made; that is, making moral judgments—whatever that may mean—is not the same as expressing a preference, and taking moral action is not the same as acting on the basis of our preferences. It is often the case that we do what we judge to be right even when we would prefer to be doing something else.

Furthermore, though morality is concerned with concepts like good and bad or right and wrong, not every use of such expressions is a moral use. For instance, we might say, "that's a good cat" and we may mean it makes a nice house pet, or it's a particularly fine example of a specific feline breed. We surely wouldn't mean that the cat has developed a fine character and acts in morally good ways. We also ordinarily use the expressions right and wrong to refer to how a particular task is performed—there is, for example, a right or wrong way to brush your teeth, but certainly not a moral or immoral way. There are non-moral uses of prescriptive language as well. For example, "This is how you should play a G chord on the guitar." Such examples point to the obvious fact that we evaluate objects of all sorts, from cats to tableware to works of art, apply standards, and prescribe courses of action in non-moral ways.

Also, there are institutions besides morality that seek to regulate human behavior; these most notably include law, religion, and manners. And though there are clearly points of convergence between them and morality, it is important to make appropriate distinctions. The law, at least in a civil society, promotes social harmony and societal well-being; it lays down standards for resolving conflicts, and prohibits actions that are harmful to others. Yet, even in this case, the law may allow certain actions that some would find morally wrong and it may simply be silent on other matters covered by moral rules. Moreover, we may judge entire legal systems as morally suspect or downright unjust. Many people derive their moral judgments from the religious beliefs they hold, but there are many different religions and hence no one conception of religious authority; morality need not derive from divine authority. That is, religion may indeed inform our moral judgments, but it is not the ultimate ground of those judgments. Clearly, non-religious persons are not motivated by following divinely issued rules, but are quite capable of being morally good individuals. Finally, systems of manners differ widely across cultural lines. In one place you might put your napkin on your lap, in another wear it like a bib; in one place you show social respect by shaking hands, in another place by bowing; or in one culture you eat with a knife and fork, in another with your hands. These mark clear differences in conventional behavior, but they do not represent deep human disagreement such as we might find when real moral difference is in play. Though it would be generally offensive according to our system of manners to eat with our hands in a fancy restaurant, we might gladly do so in some other part of the world; to use an extreme example—we likely would not be so eager to engage in cannibalism, despite another culture's acceptance of it. We wouldn't just find it distasteful from a culinary point of view; we'd find it morally unacceptable.

Everyday morality involves action and character, and moral philosophy is the systematic attempt to understand these concepts. The questions of action (what we do) and character (what kinds of persons we are) are, no doubt, interrelated. The actions we take most often reflect the kind of persons we are; or, at least, we aspire to make our actions consistent with the character traits we develop. In one important sense, this is what it means to have integrity; namely, that our actions embody and publically demonstrate our deepest convictions. Our ordinary moral experience, then, involves much more than just doing things or performing actions. Because we are reflective creatures, we think about whether our actions fit together with certain core beliefs and deeply held convictions, or whether they can be justified in terms of their attachment to known truths or likely outcomes, or whether they follow from certain fundamental moral principles. Or maybe we decide that there are no moral principles at all; that so-called moral rules are really just social conventions that are ultimately arbitrary. Or we might think that there is nothing like a human nature, just different groups and cultures that supply the norms for guiding behavior and the standards for deciding what character traits are worth having.

That said, the subject matter of moral philosophy is not limited to determining what we should or should not do, or what traits we ought to cultivate and which we should avoid. Moral philosophy is also about the nature of morality itself. Is morality relative or objective? Is it just a matter of subjective feelings or one's personal opinions? Are there such things as moral facts? Are moral judgments statements of such facts or are they really expressions of moral attitudes and emotions? Can we know our moral claims to be true or false? When we consider a course of action or we adopt a moral perspective can we be reasonably certain that we are correct? Most of us, at some time or other, have considered such questions in our ordinary moral experience. It is the task of the moral philosopher to consider them in ways that are perhaps more theoretical and systematic than we ordinarily do, but which are by no means inconsistent with our everyday morality.

Moral philosophy comprises all these sorts of questions and issues. This is apparent when we consider the standard divisions of the discipline. There are three main areas of moral philosophy: *Meta-ethics*; *normative ethics*; and *applied ethics*. Meta-ethics is that area of moral philosophy concerned with the nature or foundations of ethics itself. It is not concerned with determining the rules of right conduct or what actions are right or wrong; that is, meta-ethics is not normative. In general a meta-ethical theory seeks to describe, through careful conceptual analysis, just what it is we are doing when we engage in moral discourse, make moral judgments, have moral beliefs, or how it is we understand moral motivation, or how/whether we can justify our moral claims, or how we might determine, if possible at all, the truth or falsity of our moral claims. Specifically we might ask whether there are any universal, objectively valid moral principles or whether the standards of moral rightness are really just subjective or relative to one's culture. We might think that when we make a moral judgment we express a fact about the world; we might believe that such "judgments" are just expressions of our feelings or emotions; we might think that we are motivated to act on the basis of our beliefs or that beliefs by themselves can never motivate us to act, we need desire as well. Meta-ethics is not just one theory or one kind of theory, but rather it involves a complex nexus of conceptual concerns. It has several dimensions: Linguistic/semantic (*What do terms like 'right' and 'wrong', 'good' and 'bad' really mean?*), psychological (*What constitutes a moral motive?*), metaphysical—how morality relates to reality (*Are there such things as moral facts?*), and epistemological—how we might come to justify our moral beliefs (*Can we know whether our moral beliefs are actually true or false?*).

In this sense, meta-ethical theory is abstract, as it takes us away from moral action and asks after the why and what-for of ethics itself.

To say that meta-ethics is abstract is not to suggest that it is irrelevant to or even uncommon in our everyday moral experience. Suppose you say that it is wrong to eat meat. How might we understand this? Do you mean that it is wrong for you based on your attitudes about animals, but that it may not be wrong for someone else? This is not an uncommon view; after all there are plenty of vegetarians and carnivores who dine together without passing negative moral judgments on each other. Or do you mean that eating meat is objectively wrong in the sense that there is a reason independent of your own attitude, or that there is some property of eating meat itself which makes it so? In this sense, you might judge the meat eater as morally corrupt in some way. If that were the case, dining together would not be such a good thing. Notice what's at issue here. The difference between the two scenarios is not about the action of eating meat, since in both cases there is some sort of acceptance that *it is wrong to eat meat*. Initially the difference appears to be about interpreting the sentence, 'It is wrong to eat meat', or perhaps more precisely about how the word 'wrong' means in that sentence. But there's a lot more going on. The example illustrates not only a difference in meaning, but also differences about whether moral judgments are true or false or neither, about what motivates us, about objectivity and subjectivity, and about what constitutes a fact at all. Do you really even have a 'belief' when making a moral judgment? If, in using a sentence like 'It is wrong to eat meat', you are just expressing an attitude, then one consequence of this is that the sentence, while it looks like a statement of fact, is neither true nor false in that attitudinal expressions are not the sort of things we consider as having a truth-value. Attitudes are subjectively constituted and may have no actual relation to anything outside of you. Or you may have a genuine belief in that the sentence does have a determinate truth-value and that you think you have good reason or justification to believe it to be true. Attitudes and beliefs, then, differ in terms of their bearing on the world. So the general sense of how morality relates to the world is shaped, in large measure, by how we understand basic moral concepts.

Whereas *meta-ethics* is about the meaning of morality, *normative ethics* seeks to answer questions about what is actually good for us and which actions are, in fact, right or wrong. In order to address such questions, normative ethics focuses not on what people actually do but on what it is we ought to do. Normative ethics is action-guiding in that it attempts to develop a general theory that lays out the conditions for determining how we should lead our lives and which actions we should perform. It concerns the nature of the moral agent, the person performing actions, and considers the extent to which a person's motives and intentions matter in determining the moral value of actions. What kind of persons should we be? What are the standards used to distinguish good from bad character and what role does a person's character play in the evaluation of his or her actions? It concerns actions themselves. Are actions intrinsically right or wrong or does the rightness or wrongness of actions depend on outcomes or consequences? Are certain actions duties that we have an obligation to perform irrespective of what they bring about or do moral demands arise only in the context of particular situations?

There are three main types of normative ethical theory: *Consequentialist* theories, *deontological* or *duty-based* theories, and *virtue* theories. Consequentialist theories emphasize the idea that the rightness or wrongness of an action is determined, respectively, by the good or bad consequences that an action produces. Such theories define morally correct action in terms of a prior conception of what is good and attempt to provide a procedure for weighing the good and bad consequences of our actions. The idea is to perform actions that have the best overall outcomes, to do things that improve circumstances in the world. Deontological or duty-based theories emphasize the idea that actions are right or wrong independent of their consequences. Such theories hold that the concept of moral rightness is primary and attempt to identify the principles and criteria, or a supreme moral principle, we should employ in deciding when an action is a duty or not. Under this view, we have an obligation to perform actions which are known to be duties and to perform them without regard to their outcomes. Virtue theories focus on a person's character as the source of moral action. According to this view, we should develop those qualities of character, the virtues, that are essential for our happiness and for living well with others in the moral community. The fundamental task of moral philosophy, in this case, is to explain how we develop such traits and to understand how possessing them leads to morally correct action.

Applied ethics is that branch of moral philosophy that brings normative principles to bear on particular issues and cases. These include a whole host of problems that demand our moral attention about matters of life and death, treatment of animals, business responsibilities, the law and civic life, technology, scientific research, the environment, and so on. Is doctor-assisted suicide morally permissible? Should we use animals in experimentation? What rights do employees have in the workplace? Is affirmative action morally justifiable? Is capital punishment morally permissible? How does computer use or Internet browsing affect individual privacy? What moral standards should be employed when conducting scientific research using human beings? What obligations do we have to protect the environment and preserve resources?

Though these are undoubtedly pressing issues, this book does not offer any extended analysis of specific moral problems; instead the focus is on some of the conceptual concerns of *meta-ethics* and several leading theories in *normative ethics*. There are three reasons why the focus is on these areas. The first is that a foundation in normative ethics is required to deal with particular problems effectively. We'd be spinning our wheels if we tried to address such concerns without at least a basic understanding of some fundamental moral concepts. This work, then, attempts to provide that ground. Second, almost everyone has an opinion about specific large-scale moral issues. My contention is that if we start with the issues rather than the foundations, it will likely be the case that we come away having the same opinions. This is because we know the issues in broad outline and have probably already taken sides in the debates, say, between pro-choice and pro-life adherents, or those who favor versus those who oppose capital punishment, or those who believe we have a responsibility to aid the starving around the world and those who think our responsibilities extend only to those in our familiar circles. We frame opinions and hold them firmly in such cases. By itself, this is far from the worst thing; but that said, it is better to make judgments critically than simply to hold opinions strongly. The third reason has to do with the conditions under which we subject opinions, including and perhaps most especially our own, to some critical scrutiny and how it is we come to understand why we hold the positions we do and why we have the values we have. It may indeed be the case that, in the end, we still hold the same viewpoints, but now perhaps with an enriched sense of justification.

The chapters in this text proceed as follows: *Chapter 1* considers a common conception that all matters of morality are relative, either to an individual (subjectivism) or to a larger "culture" (cultural moral relativism). It considers further whether there really aren't any objectively valid, universal moral principles. *Chapter 2* examines another commonly held moral position, namely, egoism. The chapter begins with a discussion of *psychological egoism,* a meta-ethical theory about what actually motivates human action, and follows with a discussion of *ethical egoism,* a normative theory that suggests each person should act in his or her own best interest. *Chapter 3* deals with the question of value and what might be our ultimate good. In particular, we will critically examine the view known as *hedonism*—the idea that pleasure is the one thing that is valuable in and of itself. *Chapters 4, 5,* and *6* consider the three leading normative theories. *Chapter 4* considers consequentialism and the idea that the rightness or wrongness of an action is determined by the goodness or badness of its consequences. As a prime example of consequentialism, we will examine *utilitarianism*—the view that we ought always act in such a way so as to bring about the greatest good for the greatest number.

Chapter 5 examines *deontology* or duty-based ethics, the theory that actions are right or wrong in terms of whether they adhere to moral rules or principles and not in terms of consequences; here we will consider Kant's moral theory and his idea that, on the basis of reason alone, we can discover a universal moral principle—*the categorical imperative. Chapter 6* is about *virtue ethics*. Whereas consequentialist and deontological ethical theories are primarily concerned with identifying universal moral principles and determining how and when actions are morally right or wrong, virtue ethics is concerned more fundamentally with the development of a virtuous character. 'What is the good life?' and 'what kind of person should one be?' are the central questions of virtue ethics. Here the focus is on Aristotle's conception of happiness and his theory of virtue.

A final note: This is an introductory text, so by necessity none of the theories under consideration is treated exhaustively. That said, it is my hope that they are treated sufficiently enough to spur some further thinking about morality.

chapter 1

Relativism and Objectivism

It is a popular view to think that what is morally right and morally wrong varies from society to society, culture to culture, place to place, and perhaps even person to person. But just how is it that people come to have this view about morality and what are its consequences? Before confronting this question directly, consider the simple fact that different cultures have different customs and engage in different practices. We are frequently fascinated by the fact that the world is a richly diverse place and celebrate cultural differences in music, the arts, food, etc. and we are quaintly curious about rites and rituals that seem odd from our perspective—funeral rites, magic and medicine, holiday observances, and marriage ceremonies to name a few. Some differences strike us as innocuous—in which hands the fork and knife are held while eating, folding a napkin on your lap or wearing it like a bib, or wearing shorts with a sports coat and tie. Others strike us a bit of a nuisance—for instance, figuring out how to drive on the left when you've driven only on the right side of the road. With respect to these differences, we often see value in the old adage, "when in Rome, do as the Romans do," and might add "when in Coney Island, eat a Nathan's hotdog."

We don't fret about these cultural differences and, in fact, think they make the world a more interesting and dynamic place. The fundamental reason why we are not troubled by the kinds of differences alluded to above is because there is really no moral issue at stake. We don't argue, for instance, that it's simply wrong to drive on the left side of the road and claim to have discovered some objective, rational principle from which such a judgment could be derived. We simply follow the rules of the road in whatever country we happen to be. But what happens when we do consider another class of differences—differences which are marked not by celebration, interest, or curiosity, but rather by deep moral disagreement? Here we might believe that there is some objective standard or principle on the basis of which we could settle our moral disagreement; but, as we will see, that is precisely what is at issue here.

Consider cases where the difference in behavior of members of one society to another reflects a deeper difference in the values each society accepts and the standards employed in the determination of what qualifies as morally acceptable action in each culture. A particularly striking case is that of female genital circumcision, commonly referred to as female genital mutilation (FGM) by the many who oppose the practice. In certain African, Middle Eastern, and Indonesian societies the practice of female genital circumcision—the complete or partial removal of the external female genitalia or even sewing the vagina closed (only to be opened for intercourse and childbirth and then sewn closed again)—is either prescribed or, at least, permissible. Such procedures are routinely and forcibly performed on young girls and young women, rendering them incapable of feeling sexual pleasure, committing them to a life of pain, and making them prone to a range of life-threatening infections. There are no discernible health benefits to the practice; it is only harmful.

How do we respond to this sort of case? Is the response modeled on that which we have toward the other kind of cultural differences noted above? That is, do we simply accept it as another difference in culture that makes the world an interesting place? It's hard to imagine that anyone would apply the "when in Rome" principle here. Instead it seems that reasonable people would be more inclined to make the judgment that this practice is not simply a matter of cultural difference, but that it is barbaric and ought to outlawed. Yet there are those who argue that although we wouldn't engage in such a practice, we are in no position to judge others as morally wrong for doing so.

While some cultural differences are morally neutral, others place us squarely in the realm of moral discourse. The philosophical matter is one about the very nature of morality itself: In making moral judgments can we rightly appeal to an objective moral principle, a standard that crosses cultural boundaries, or are moral principles themselves to be understood only within the context of a particular culture or society? This chapter examines two competing positions, *moral relativism* and *moral objectivism* and outlines arguments for and against each of these theories. It is best to start with basic definitions. *Moral objectivism* is the view that there are objectively valid moral principles or standards that apply to all persons in the determination of what is morally right or wrong; accordingly, there are such things as objective moral facts. *Moral relativism* denies both the idea that there are principles which are objectively applicable to all persons and the claim that moral facts are objective; if there are such things as moral facts at all, then even they shift from culture to culture (or perhaps even from individual to individual). The moral relativist holds that what is morally right or morally wrong depends on standards that are normative in some particular context or other.

Moral Relativism

There is a distinction between an empirical or factual claim and a normative claim about what is right and wrong. An empirical or factual claim is a judgment about the way things are. A normative claim is a judgment about how things ought to be. The term *relativism* can be used in either sense. On the one hand it refers to the indisputable fact that different societies have different moral codes. It is just a fact that, in some societies, female genital circumcision is allowed and in others, it is prohibited. What is thought to be right in one society is believed to be wrong in another. For the sake of convenience, this view is referred to here as *cultural relativism. Cultural relativism* is the descriptive or empirical theory that different cultures have different conceptions of what is morally right or morally wrong. The relativity of moral practices is simply a brute sociological or anthropological fact. By itself this theory, though often used as part of an argument in defense of moral relativism, makes no additional claims as to what the nature of morality is. It is a fact that, in certain African cultures, female genital circumcision is morally permissible and that in the United States it is considered morally wrong. *Moral relativism*, in contrast, is the normative view that moral rightness and moral wrongness are themselves relative to particular cultures or individuals. This comes down to saying that whatever a culture or person holds to be right or wrong **is** right or wrong for that culture or person; that is, rightness and wrongness are defined by what a person or group of persons happens to think is right or wrong. In saying this much, the moral relativist denies that we can give an objective account of morality. Beyond simply pointing to factual differences between, say, certain African cultures and the United States, the moral relativist holds that in certain African cultures, female genital circumcision is (not merely thought to be) morally permissible and in the United States it is (and not merely thought to be) morally wrong. So, for the moral relativist, the same action is both right and wrong; it just depends on where one is, what group one belongs to, and what set of norms one follows. This chapter is concerned fundamentally with this sense of relativism.

Another way of couching the difference between cultural and moral relativism is to distinguish between the *diversity thesis* and the *dependency thesis*. Cultural relativism adopts the *diversity thesis*, which states simply that there is factual variability among different cultures as to what counts as morally right and morally wrong, and on the basis of this factual circumstance it accepts the further fact that there is apparently no one, universal moral standard or set of moral principles to which all cultures appeal. Notice the diversity thesis doesn't deny that there is such a standard; it only makes the more attenuated claim that different cultures don't rely on one moral standard. This thesis is distinguished from the stronger and more controversial *dependency thesis*, which states that whether a person's actions are right or wrong depends on the cultural context in which one acts. Under the dependency thesis, morality itself is relative to cultures and so there **really** is no universal moral standard. The dependency thesis thus expressly denies the existence of an objective moral standard that is cross-culturally normative. This is the fundamental idea of moral relativism.[1]

There are several arguments, varying in degrees of strength and complexity that are used in defense of moral relativism. A particularly simple argument is one that the moral philosopher, James Rachels, names the *Cultural Differences Argument*.[2] Take the example of female genital circumcision. The argument goes like this:

1. Members of certain African and Middle Eastern societies believe that female genital circumcision is morally permissible; Americans believe that it is morally wrong.
2. Therefore, female genital circumcision is neither objectively right nor objectively wrong. It is only a matter of what one believes, which varies from culture to culture.

This is an instance of the general argument that, as per Rachels, goes this way:

1. Different cultures have different moral codes.
2. Therefore, there is no objective moral truth. What is morally right and morally wrong are matters of what one believes, which varies from culture to culture.

What this argument is really saying is that cultural relativism implies moral relativism, or put yet another way: We can deduce the dependency thesis from the diversity thesis. From the fact that there are cultural differences, it follows that morality cannot be objective. The obvious problem with this argument is that the conclusion simply doesn't follow from the premise. It is an uncontroversial fact that different cultures have different moral codes, that the diversity thesis is true, but only knowing that much doesn't commit us to the truth of moral relativism. We know it is a fact that different cultures have different moral codes, so the premise is true. At the same time it is quite possible that it is false that there are no objective moral truths; that is the conclusion could be false. This is sufficient to demonstrate that the argument is invalid. The logical notion of validity says that in a valid argument, if the premises are true, then the conclusion **must** be true.

Let's look at it another way by constructing an argument that has the same form as the Cultural Differences Argument. Consider the following analogous argument:

1. Members of *alpha* society believe that the moon is made of Swiss cheese, members of *beta* society believe that the moon is not made of Swiss cheese.
2. Therefore, there is no objective truth about what the moon is or is not made of. It is only a matter of what one believes, which varies from society to society.

Suppose that the statement about the *alpha* and *beta* societies is true. It is plainly evident here that the conclusion doesn't follow. It is certainly objectively true that whatever the moon is made of, it is not made of Swiss cheese, so 2 is clearly false. Some beliefs are just downright wrong; in this case, completely preposterous. Why couldn't the same be said for the moral relativism argument? It may be possible that some moral beliefs are just plain wrong as well. The Cultural Differences Argument attempts to draw a conclusion about objective moral truth based on what people happen to believe, but this works no better for morality than it does for the moon. As Rachels points out, none of this demonstrates that moral relativism is false; all it has shown is that the Cultural Differences Argument is not a good logical argument, and so consequently ought to be rejected as a defense of moral relativism.[3]

Another approach that is commonly taken in defense of moral relativism has to do with the sort of attitudes we should adopt with respect to cultures other than our own. Many moral relativists believe that relativism is necessary in order to avoid *eth-*

nocentrism. Ethnocentrism is the view that one's own culture is superior to other cultures, with no other evidence than that it is one's own culture. Basically the ethnocentrist says, "My morality is better than yours because it's my morality." Clearly this is an arbitrary position in that it makes no appeal to any independent standard that could be used to substantiate its claim. In this sense, it is a prejudicial posture much like that of racism and sexism, and so ought to be avoided. In this much, we could agree with the relativist.

The more important issue is whether one actually needs to embrace moral relativism in order to demonstrate that there is something wrong with ethnocentrism. Is it really the case that any non-relativistic position must by necessity embrace ethno-centrism? Is any claim that one morality is superior to another an instance of ethnocentric prejudice? Think about cultures that advocate genocide or terrorism. One could reasonably argue that a culture that values safety, liberty, and freedom of expression, indeed a culture that values human life, is morally superior to a culture that supports instilling fear, killing innocent civilians, or exterminating an entire race of people. And one could make such an argument without fear of being labeled ethnocentric. That is, a person might believe that there is a non-biased principle—for example, it is wrong to purposefully kill the innocent—that sup-plies a ground for such a judgment. In this case, one would not merely be asserting his cultural superiority but would claim that there is an objective reason for making the moral appraisal. The relativist might respond by saying that the principle itself is just another cultural posit. But that would be to miss the point. The point here is not whether there actually are such objective stan-dards or principles, but rather that the appeal to a principle as a justifying reason is just what is meant by being unbiased. This is a different sort of intellectual activity than simply proclaiming the correctness of your own moral views. So there is a meaningful difference between ethnocentrism and moral justification. Even the relativist should be able to admit that much, and if that's the case, then even the relativist would have to admit that some non-relativists—those who at least believe that the principles to which they appeal are objective and provide what they take to be unbiased reasons—are not being ethnocentric. Such non-relativists would, in fact, find ethnocentrism morally objectionable.

Another positive conception of moral relativism hinges on the attitude of tolerance. To be tolerant is to be willing to accept the fact that others may have views quite different from our own and to respect that difference. Tolerance doesn't mean that we should embrace the views of others, only that we allow them to hold their views and act on them, without any negative judgment or interference on our part. It is easy to see how and why some believe that moral relativism and the attitude of tolerance go hand-in-hand. Each culture has its own morality and each lets the other live out that morality in the practices it respectively allows or prohibits.

There is a standard argument, the tolerance argument, which is often proposed as a defense of moral relativism. The argument can be framed as follows:

1. If there are no objective measures for comparing and evaluating different cultural moralities, then it would seem we have no basis for criticizing other moralities.
2. There are no objective moral measures for comparing and evaluating different cultural moralities. (This assumes the truth of the fundamental claim of moral relativism; namely that there are no objectively valid moral principles.)
3. Therefore, we have no basis for criticizing other moralities.
4. If we have no basis for criticizing other moralities, then we should just accept the difference and respect other cultures for what they are (that is, we should be tolerant of other cultures).
5. Therefore, we should always be tolerant of other cultures.

This is a stronger argument than the Cultural Differences Argument. In the first place, from a purely logical perspective, it's a valid argument. That is, if the premises are true, then the conclusion would have to be true as well. Moreover, the argument rests on an attitude that many people find appealing. The idea of tolerance involves notions like respect, restraint, and non-interference, all of which are generally deemed to be worthy traits to cultivate.

Despite its apparent strength, the argument may fail, in certain salient respects, to provide an adequate defense of moral relativism. Consider two distinct questions: 1) What if it is not true that we should always be tolerant of other cultures? That is, what if the conclusion of the tolerance argument is false? Then something has gone awry somewhere in the premises. 2) What if it is true that we should be tolerant of other cultures? Then it might be the case that relativism cannot hold to its fundamental idea that there are no objective moral truths or principles. Let's take these in order.

The first question has to do with the limits of tolerance. Tolerance is often reasonably exercised among those who share a set of moral assumptions and between cultures with differing moral perspectives when there are moral disagreements that don't negatively affect our general sense that those with whom we disagree, other persons or cultures, are basically morally decent. For example, some people are more generous than others; some cultures encourage greater self-directed than altruistic action; some people are vegetarians, others eat meat; some cultures are more sexually permissive than others. Ordinarily we don't, and shouldn't, take such moral differences as occasions for outright condemnation of other persons or societies. We might attempt to settle the differences, but if we find that it is not possible to do so, we live with such disagreements. In other words, we find them tolerable. It's not that such disagreements aren't morally significant or that they effectively reduce to the kind of differences signaled by a variety of morally neutral individual preferences or cultural practices, rather it's that they don't cut deep enough to warrant profoundly negative moral judgments about others.

Some societies, with a presumed moral imperative, sponsor terror, commit genocide, mutilate the bodies of young women, or shoot young girls just for attending school. Should we apply the same reasoning about tolerance in such cases? Here, despite having other disagreements of the sort mentioned above, different individuals and cultures could agree that these actions are just the kind of actions that we ought not to tolerate. The agreement may not be merely a contingent matter. It's not simply that we happen to agree, but rather that we agree in substance about the nature of such actions or the moralities that lead to them and judge that there is something evil about them. For that reason, we find such actions intolerable.

We need not, then, accept the moral relativist's conclusion, as in the argument from tolerance, that we should always be tolerant of other cultures. For though we might accept the fact that persons in other cultures have some reason to act based on the moralities that are normative for them, it is the case that there are overriding trans-cultural reasons that trump, as it were, the more local ones. The idea, for instance, that there is something evil about certain actions crosses cultural boundaries as evidenced by the fact that otherwise different cultures may share that judgment. In short, it is here that we bump up against the limits of tolerance.[4]

So one counter-argument to the tolerance defense of moral relativism suggests that there is a reason for believing that it's not the case that we should always be tolerant of other cultures. If this is so, then it follows that the central claim of relativism—that there are no objective moral principles—is questionable as well. The argument could be constructed this way: The moral relativist believes that if we have no basis for criticizing other moralities, then we should always be tolerant of other moralities. But if it's not the case that we should always be tolerant of other moralities, then it's not the case that we have no basis for criticizing them. There may indeed be a basis on which we can criticize other moralities. The relativist believes further that if there are no objective moral principles, then we have no basis for criticizing other moralities. But we do have a basis for criticizing other moralities. It follows that there are objective moral principles, those available to persons of different cultural backgrounds, which may serve as the basis for such criticism.

Suppose this is all simply wrong-headed and that it is, in fact, true that we should always be tolerant of other moralities. Does moral relativism fare any better under this circumstance? This is precisely what the second question above asks us to consider. There is a straightforward problem for the relativist here. Relativism, of course, denies that there are any objective moral principles applicable to all cultural moralities. At the same time it says that we ought to be tolerant of other moralities. It seems, then, that tolerance is a principle that all cultures should embrace and that the moral relativist actually does recommend the acceptance, by all cultures, of an objective principle. It would follow that any culture that is intolerant violates that principle. It wouldn't help the relativist to say that tolerance itself is relative to particular cultural moralities, as that would make the tolerance argument impossible from the start. Some moralities would be tolerant and others would not. To say that those that are tolerant would have to tolerate the intolerant and those that are intolerant would have to tolerate the tolerant just doesn't make sense. So either the principle of tolerance is relative or it is objective. But it can't be relative; that leads to an absurdity. The principle of tolerance must, then, be objective. But if the principle of tolerance is objective, then the fundamental claim of relativism that there are no objective moral principles must be false. Moral relativism, according to this argument, is self-defeating.

Though it seemed initially that there is an easy connection made between moral relativism and tolerance, it now appears it's not such an easy one after all. Moral relativism, in its effort to portray itself as a fair-minded moral stance, may have simply planted the seeds of its own demise. In sum, it can neither accept nor reject the principle that we should always be tolerant of other moralities. If we reject it, then we have a basis for criticizing other cultures; if we accept it, then we are appealing to an objective standard. In either case, relativism is impossible.

Some might suggest that moral relativism could be salvaged by replacing the attitude of tolerance with one of indifference, but that would be no foundation on which to build a moral theory, since morality, by definition, involves making judgments.[5] Indifference, at best, is the attitude of refraining or abstaining from making judgments; perhaps more than that it is the attitude of not caring or disregard. Morality requires, for instance, that we don't merely shut our eyes to atrocities, but that we condemn them. To embrace indifference, in virtue of its disregard, would be to give up on morality altogether. Worse yet, indifference is the breeding ground of *ethnocentrism*, the very view moral relativism is designed to combat in the first place.

Subjectivism

Subjectivism is a form of moral relativism that says morality is not relative to cultures, but rather that it is relative to each individual person. In this sense, morality is not a set of conventional norms that are shared by members of a group, it is simply whatever an individual happens to believe. Moral rightness and moral wrongness are themselves defined by what any individual happens to believe is right or wrong. So what is wrong for me may be right for you, and what is wrong for you may be right for me. Subjectivism is fueled by the fact that there are many moral issues on which people disagree. Consider, for instance, the following common disagreements having to do with life or death matters:

i) John believes capital punishment is morally permissible; Jerry thinks it is morally wrong and ought to be prohibited.

ii) Jane believes that abortion is morally permissible and should be a matter of personal choice; Mary believes abortion is a form of murder.

iii) Reggie believes that some wars are just and that it is morally permissible to kill in a just war; Archie is a pacifist and thinks that all war is evil.

iv) Ira enjoys a thick steak and thinks it is perfectly fine to kill animals for food; Sandy is a vegetarian and thinks it is wrong to kill animals under any circumstance.

Each of these cases represents an instance of real moral disagreement. But what is it that the persons involved are really disagreeing about? Clearly, these sorts of disagreements are about specific moral issues. Subjectivism, however, pushes further to the idea that each individual has his/her own sense of rightness and wrongness. Is that really sensible? It is one thing to disagree about specific moral issues, quite a different matter to suggest that morality itself is relative to individuals.

Putting aside the obvious fact that subjectivism, like conventional moral relativism, implies that one action is both right and wrong depending on who happens to believe what, there is a more subtle difficulty with this view. The problem has to do with the meaning of our moral language. Take the case of abortion. Jane believes abortion is morally permissible and Mary believes it is not morally permissible. They clearly disagree about abortion, but they don't (and really can't disagree) about what it means to say that abortion (or any act for that matter) is right or wrong. Something that is morally wrong is, by definition, something that ought not be done. The meaning of "morally wrong" is not itself subjectively determined.

There are indeed differences of opinion as to whether an act is wrong, but not a difference of opinion about the concept of wrongness itself. To illustrate, let's look at three different sentences:

1. Abortion is murder.
2. Abortion is not murder.
3. Murder is the unjustifiable killing of another person.

The first two sentences reflect a difference of opinion about abortion. So far so good; but what if one says, "I disagree with sentence number 3; murder is, in my opinion, perfectly justifiable. You might think that murder is morally wrong, but I think it is morally permissible." The fact here is that such a person simply doesn't know the meaning of the word "murder." If an action is permissible, it is justifiable; that is, there is a reason one could give, where that reason is enough to warrant performing the action. If an action is wrong, there is no reason sufficient enough to justify performing that action. The third sentence is a definition, whereas the first and second express judgments that are based on that definition but are not themselves definitions. So if some form of killing is justifiable, then by definition it isn't murder. This doesn't, of course, settle the disagreement about abortion. It only shows what kind of disagreement it is—one about whether abortion is or is not justifiable. In order to see this much, we already have to agree on something, in this case, the definition of murder.

The general point here is that our individual subjective judgments about particular actions depend upon the acceptance of other judgments that are not subjectively determined. Here's where the spade turns for subjectivism. The condition that makes our particular moral judgments possible and intelligible is the acceptance of a certain class of moral claims that have shared inter-subjective linguistic meaning. We cannot, without eschewing the idea of meaningful language altogether, say that moral wrongness and moral rightness themselves are matters of individual belief. Irrespective of our differences of opinion about issues like capital punishment, abortion, war, or the killing of animals, we don't disagree about what moral wrongness and moral rightness are. Put positively, we agree on these concepts because our language, objective as it is, requires it. Unless we are prepared to admit that such concepts are not part of moral discourse—which seems patently absurd—we can reject the idea that morality itself is subjective.

Moral Objectivism

The central claim of moral relativism, as we have seen, is that there are no objective moral principles or standards that apply to all persons. According to moral relativism, morality is just a matter of what a culture or an individual person happens to think is morally right or wrong. Moral objectivism stands in direct opposition to relativism in that it claims that there are objective principles that apply to all persons independent of their cultural context or personal beliefs and that there are such things as moral facts. The moral objectivist argues that such principles should guide our actions in any context and serve to justify our moral judgments. If it could be demonstrated that there were even one such principle, then moral relativism would be false, since relativism denies that there are any such principles at all. There may, in fact, be many universally valid moral principles.[6]

Louis Pojman notes that it is important, in the first instance, to distinguish between moral *objectivism* and moral *absolutism*. Moral absolutism is the view that universal moral principles are such that they should never be violated no matter what the circumstances, whereas a more moderate moral objectivism takes the position that moral principles are generally binding but not absolute in the sense that they be overridden—not willy-nilly, but in terms of applying another firm principle that takes precedence in some circumstance or other. From the absolutist perspective, moral principles obtain in every circumstance; that is, no moral principle can be overridden by any other.[7] In his account of moral objectivism, Pojman appeals to our basic moral intuitions and, following the moral philosopher W. D. Ross, writes:

> On the objectivist's account moral principles are what William Ross refers to as *prima facie* principles, valid rules of action which should generally be adhered to, but which may be overridden by another moral principle in cases of moral conflict. For example, while a principle of justice may generally outweigh a principle of benevolence, there are times when enormous good could be done by sacrificing a small amount of justice, so that an objectivist would be more inclined to act according to the principle of benevolence.[8]

One problem with the absolutist view is that moral principles invariably come into conflict and there would be no way to settle that conflict if we could not reasonably decide on what principle to apply when. Take, for example, the common view that it is wrong to lie. In general we hold to this principle and might do so for several reasons—truth-telling is a condition for trust; people deserve the truth because they are rationally competent and can distinguish truth from falsity; lying is a form of dishonesty, etc. But what if lying to a would-be murderer was necessary to save the life of an innocent person. Don't we intuitively believe it would be correct to do so? Why so? It would seem that we've made a reasonable judgment that in such a circumstance the general prohibition against lying may be overridden by another moral principle, something to the effect that we ought always do what we can, when and where we can, to protect the life of an innocent person. The point here is that we needn't sacrifice objectivity when absolutism fails.

Favoring this more moderate approach to moral objectivism actually strengthens the case against moral relativism. Moral relativists often argue that any affirmation of objective moral principles amounts to embracing moral absolutism and absolutism is wrong because it disallows for any variability in terms of moral actions. If, however, it is possible to have moral objectivity without being committed to the idea that no principle can be overridden, then the moral relativist is simply wrong in assuming that the denial of relativism amounts to the affirmation of absolutism. Moral relativism and moderate moral objectivism could agree, then, that moral absolutism is not an acceptable theory. That being said, the moral relativist would be faced with the much more difficult challenge of having to show that certain basic intuitions about what is generally morally right and morally wrong have no objective validity whatsoever.

Moral objectivism doesn't only seek to settle moral conflicts. More important, it provides a theoretical framework for justifying our intuitive moral beliefs, which beliefs constitute a set of core moral principles that guide our own behavior and supply a ground for criticizing the behavior of others. It's not that we should think of these principles as applying only to ourselves and our own judgments, but rather that they are precisely the kinds of principles that any rational thinking moral person would accept. Take the following extreme example: Suppose you encountered a society that engaged in the practice of using babies as footballs. Would we really be going out on a limb in suggesting that "it is morally wrong to use babies as footballs" is a principle that applies to all reasonable moral agents? The likelihood is that you would find the practice horrific. This should signal the fact that it is more reasonable to suppose that such a society is morally corrupt than that you should question the objective validity of the moral principle. Does it really matter whether that society accepts the practice, as the moral relativist would have to say? It's difficult to imagine any circumstance that would warrant our revising the principle sufficiently to accommodate those whose moral perspective is so wildly opposed to what we consider reasonable. We are, in fact, more likely to judge such behavior as "perverse, ignorant, or irrational" and infer that those who perform such actions are "morally deficient, morally blind, ignorant, or irrational" than to suppose that non-acceptance of the principle is an indication that the principle itself is not true or objective.[9] Further, it would make no difference if we discovered why the society believed it was permissible to use babies as footballs. This is the case because our understanding of the principle—"it is wrong to use babies as footballs"—is not bound by a set of cultural values but is delivered in terms of basic human sensibility.

Matters are, of course, somewhat different when we consider less extreme examples. Take the basic moral belief that it is wrong to steal. Here we allow for a considerable degree of variability in terms of what particular acts count as stealing. Different societies have different conceptions of property and entitlement; even within one's own culture there are varying conceptions of what is yours and what others have a right to take or not. Even though we adjust the applicability of the principle depending on those sorts of differences, we don't eschew the principle altogether. The notion of moral objectivity entails that there be a core morality, not that the principles that constitute that core are everywhere accorded the same ranking or are applied in exactly the same way.[10]

This core morality comprises a set of objective principles which are, as Pojman puts it, "minimally basic" in that they are those that are "necessary for the good life," those required for living a flourishing life and living well with others. He provides a list of ten such principles, not necessarily complete or ordered in terms of importance but which lay out minimum requirements of the moral life.[11] These are:

i) Do not kill innocent people.

ii) Do not cause unnecessary pain or suffering.

iii) Do not cheat or steal.

iv) Keep your promises and honor your contracts.

v) Do not deprive another person of his or her freedom.

vi) Do justice, treating equals equally and unequals unequally.

vii) Tell the truth.

viii) Help other people, at least when the cost to oneself is minimal.

ix) Reciprocate and show gratitude.

x) Obey just laws.

We might expand this list to include other prohibitions (e.g., do not be cruel to animals) and moral demands like cultivating your own talents or developing virtuous states of character (e.g., courage, benevolence, generosity, temperance, etc.). The point remains, in any case, that there are certain fundamental guidelines that any person ought to follow if he or she is to lead a moral life, irrespective of the cultural context in which one acts.

It is not enough simply to make this assertion. It is incumbent upon the moral objectivist to provide reasons for why we ought to accept these principles and guide our actions accordingly. There are two distinct but related arguments that could be put forward in this regard: *The needs argument* and *purpose argument*. These are distinct in that each focuses on a specific morally significant aspect of human life, and each argument can be understood as addressing a particular question: 1) *What do we need?* 2) *Why do we act?* The arguments are related in that they both assume that there is a common human nature, defined respectively by a common set of needs and interests or basic human goods to be achieved.

The *needs argument* is grounded in the idea that because there is a common human nature, there are certain salient human needs, interests, and desires that we share in common. Moral principles derive from an examination of such human saliencies and are rationally designed to promote them. Those moral principles that promote our common needs, interests, and desires are objectively valid moral principles. If there is a common human nature, then there are objectively valid moral principles that apply to all human beings. Pojman frames the argument this way:

1. Human nature is relatively similar in essential respects, having a common set of needs and interests.
2. Moral principles are functions of human needs and interests, instituted by reason in order to promote the most significant needs and interests of rational beings (and perhaps others).
3. Some moral principles will promote human interests and meet human needs better than others.
4. Those principles which will meet essential needs and promote the most significant interests of humans in optimal ways can be said to be objectively valid moral principles.
5. Therefore, since there is a common human nature, there is an objectively valid set of moral principles, applicable to all humanity. [12]

The argument so designed is meant to provide a reason for accepting a set of minimally basic moral principles. It also shows one of the deepest consequences of moral relativism. If there is a common human nature, then there are objectively valid moral principles. But the moral relativist denies that there are any objectively valid moral principles and in doing so denies also that there is a common human nature.

The *purpose argument* seeks to answer the question *why do we act?* The question is not about a person's motivation, but about the goal of one's actions. Further, the idea of a goal here doesn't mean whatever satisfies any desire one might have but rather refers to a set of fundamental goods that are rooted in human nature and knowable immediately through a rational reflection on what it means to be human. Borrowing from the contemporary natural law theorist, John Finnis, we can identify a set of basic goods that are necessary for our well-being. Finnis includes the following:

i) Life—every aspect of life that matters in our ability to be self-determining: Bodily health, mental stability, relative freedom from pain and suffering, etc.

ii) Knowledge—not merely as a means to an end, but as end in itself.

iii) Play—engaging in actions enjoyable in themselves.

iv) Aesthetic Experience—the appreciation of beauty.

v) Sociability/Friendship—ranging from minimal collaboration required for a harmonious existence with others to full friendship where each acts for the sake of the other.

vi) Practical Reasonableness—the ability to use one's own intelligence in choosing one's course in life, both in terms of the actions one takes and the character one frames for oneself.

vii) Religion—the idea that there might be a transcendent origin to the order of things beyond us with which we would align our experiences so that our lives are in an alignment with order of all things. [13]

The awareness of these basic goods as those which should be pursued is not derived from any empirical investigation into the behavior of other cultures, but the rational awareness of them is a condition for the ability "to sympathetically (though not uncritically) see the point of actions, life-styles, characters, and cultures that one would not choose for oneself."[14] By itself this is not a moral judgment, but it does indicate that the awareness of such basic goods is normative in the sense that it serves as a ground for deciding what sort of life one would or should choose for oneself.

Without questioning whether this is an exhaustive list of basic human goods, or whether there are goods listed here that are not universal, or even whether there are such goods at all, let's consider an argument that assumes that human nature is defined by some such set of basic goods that are rationally knowable and worth pursuing in themselves. Objectively valid moral principles, in this instance, are derived from the practical consideration of how best to achieve those goods. The argument could be framed as follows:

1. Human nature is defined by a set of basic goods that are necessary for our well-being.
2. Human beings, on the basis of reflective reason, can know those basic goods.
3. These goods ought to be pursued.
4. Moral principles are derived from practical consideration of how best to achieve those goods.
5. Moral principles that enable us to achieve fundamental human goods are objectively valid.
6. Therefore, if there are basic goods necessary for our well-being, then there are objectively valid moral principles.

It is easy to see how certain moral principles are directly derivable from a consideration of some basic good. For instance, if life is a good that ought to be pursued, then it clearly follows that the core morality should include prohibitions against killing the innocent or inflicting needless pain and suffering. The derivation of other principles will require a more strenuous exercise in moral reasoning; how, for instance, we could derive a moral principle that requires gratitude and reciprocal action from the good of friendship. Others still will demand that we allow for some measure of voluntary determination as to how one leads one's life with the limitation that none of the basic goods is compromised. In general, the moral principles that are derived from these goods constitute a core morality in that they—to borrow again from Finnis—"lay down for us the outlines of everything one could reasonably want to do, to have, and to be."[15]

Here again, we can see the broader effects of moral relativism. In denying that there are any objectively valid moral principles, as we have seen, the relativist seemingly has to deny that there is a common human nature. In denying that there is a common human nature, moral relativism also denies that there are any naturally common human needs and interests or any fundamental human goods. Any commonality of needs or goods, would, from an internal perspective, have to be the result of a shared set of culturally contextualized values; and any agreement that crosses cultural boundaries would be a mere contingency. Moral objectivism, in contrast, provides a ground for criticizing the cultural value systems and actions of others—a ground for asserting, for instance, that female genital mutilation is downright evil—and legitimizes our moral desire that each person be given the opportunity to lead a flourishing life.

ENDNOTES

1. See Louis P. Pojman, "A Defense of Ethical Objectivisim" in *Moral Philosophy: A Reader* (4th edition) Louis P. Pojman and Peter Tramel, eds. (Hackett Publishing Company, 2009), pp. 38–52.
2. Stuart Rachels, *The Elements of Moral Philosophy* eighth edition (McGraw Hill, 2015), pp. 18–20.
3. *Ibid,* p. 20.
4. For an alternative view see Gilbert Harmon, "A Defense of Ethical Relativism" in *Moral Philosophy* Pojman and Tramel, eds. pp. 53–59. There Harmon argues that cannibals, for instance, have no reason not to eat human flesh; their morality is different from ours which prohibits eating human flesh. On that basis we might make judgments about their entire morality, but because we do not share their reasons for acting, we would not be able to judge the cannibals as morally wrong.

5. See Steven Lukes, *Moral Relativism* (Picador, 2008), pp. 39–40.

6. Pojman, "A Defense of Ethical Objectivism," p. 47.

7. Pojman, p. 47

8. Pojman, p. 47. See also W.D. Ross, *The Right and the Good* (Oxford University Press, 1931), p. 18ff.

9. Pojman, p. 47.

10. Pojman, p. 48.

11. Pojman, p. 48.

12. Pojman, p. 48.

13. See John Finnis, *Natural Law and Natural Rights* (Second Edition (Oxford University Press, 2011), pp. 85–97.

14. Finnis, p. 85.

15. Finnis, p. 97.

STUDY QUESTIONS

1. Explain the difference between *cultural relativism* and *moral relativism*.

2. Distinguish between the *diversity thesis* and the *dependency thesis*.

3. What is the *Cultural Differences Argument*?

4. What is *ethnocentrism*?

5. What is the *Tolerance Argument* in support of moral relativism?

6. What is *subjectivism*?

7. Define *moral objectivism*.

8. What is the idea of a core morality? What does Pojman mean by a "minimally basic" set of moral principles? Give examples of such principles.

9. What is the *needs argument* in support of moral objectivism? In his argument, Pojman appeals to the notion of a common human nature. How so?

10.   What is the *purpose argument*? What is Finnis's idea of a basic human good? What specific goods does he identify?

QUESTIONS FOR REFLECTION

1.   Do you think that morality is relative or objective? Give reasons for your answer.

2.   Can we legitimately judge the actions of persons in other cultures as morally wrong? Can we judge persons in other cultures as morally bad? Why or why not? Illustrate with examples of your own.

3.   Evaluate the following idea: "What's right is whatever is right for me, even though what's right for me may be wrong for you."

SUGGESTIONS FOR FURTHER READING

Benedict, Ruth. *Patterns of Culture*. Boston, MA: Houghton Mifflin, 1994.

Blackburn, Simon. *Being Good: A Short Introduction to Ethics*. New York: Oxford University Press, 2001.

Boghossian, Peter. "The Maze of Moral Relativism." *The New York Times*, July 24, 2011.

Harman, Gilbert. *The Nature of Morality: An Introduction to Ethics*. New York: Oxford University Press, 1977.

Lukes, Steven. *Moral Relativism*. New York: Picador, 2008.

Moser, Paul K., and Carson, Thomas L. (eds.). *Moral Relativism: A Reader*. New York: Oxford University Press, 2000.

Nussbaum, Martha C. "Judging Other Cultures: The Case of Genital Mutilation," in Nussbaum, *Sex and Social Justice*. New York: Oxford University Press, 1999.

Williams, Bernard. "The Truth in Relativism," in Williams, *Moral Luck*. Cambridge, UK: Cambridge University Press, 1981.

Williams, Bernard. *Ethics and the Limits of Philosophy*. Cambridge, MA: Harvard University Press, 1985.

chapter 2

Egoism

The idea that human beings always do, or perhaps should, look out exclusively for themselves is the basic point of egoism. Most people think that the moral point of view requires, to some extent, that we consider the interest and feelings of others when we decide to take a certain action. But why should we adopt that point of view at all? What if we are simply hardwired to act for our own benefit? In that case, the so-called moral point of view would be illusory. Or what if we are morally required to consider only our own interests when acting? In this regard, there would be something seriously wrong about the common moral belief that we ought to take the interests of others into account when we act.

Are we so constituted by nature such that we are motivated to act exclusively in our own interests? And even if it were possible to act in regards to the interests of others, should we do so? These two questions set into relief the distinction between two forms of egoism: *Psychological egoism* and *ethical egoism*. *Psychological egoism* is a descriptive, empirical theory about what compels us to act in the way we do. Its fundamental thesis is that, appearances to the contrary, human beings always act or are motivated to act exclusively in their own interests. The claim purports to be a factual one; that is, human action by its very nature is self-directed. It would follow, then, that altruistic action—action taken in regard to the interests of others—is simply not possible. *Ethical egoism* is a normative theory about how we should act; it claims that what we ought to do is act exclusively in our own interest. Whereas psychological egoism denies that it is even possible to act altruistically, ethical egoism recognizes the possibility of acting in the interest of others but advocates that it is really not morally acceptable to do so.

Psychological Egoism

What would the world be like if it were true that human beings couldn't help but act exclusively in their own best interests? The great English political philosopher Thomas Hobbes (1588–1679) gave a particularly striking answer to this question. Hobbes argued that human beings are selfish by nature and, as such, always pursue their own interests. We act only to secure our own satisfaction and to avoid harm. In nature everyone is equal in the tendency to want self-satisfaction, but not equal in the capacity to achieve satisfaction. The problem is that there will inevitably be conflicts of interest and so the world is one in which we would live in a constant state of insecurity, uncertainty, and fear—persistently worried that the interests of others might prevail over our own. Each person is, in some sense, at war with everyone else, and only the strongest will prevail.

Because our energies would be directed towards outdoing everyone else, little or nothing could be accomplished in such a world. All those aspects of a human life that require attention and energetic pursuit and seemingly provide our lives with value would, for all intents and purposes, be impossible. Hobbes writes that:

> In such condition, there is no place for industry; because the fruit thereof is uncertain: and consequently no culture of the earth; no navigation nor use of the commodities that may be imported by sea; no commodious building; no instruments of moving and removing, such things as require much force; no knowledge of the face of the earth; no account of time; no arts; no letters; no society . . .[1]

Hobbes concludes that life in our natural state would thus be "*solitary, poor, nasty, brutish, and short.*"

This picture of human nature seems to leave little room for moral concerns. Hobbes himself recognized this and argued that in the state of nature, the state of constant conflicting interests, there is no sense of right or wrong, good or bad, justice or injustice. Moral concepts have significance only in the context of a regulated, rule-governed community of like-minded persons; even the most ordinary moral concepts could not be derived from human nature alone. But if human nature is defined in terms of self-interest, why should we be moral at all? Why would we agree to follow rules that require us to act in ways that seemingly benefit others? The only consistent answer a psychological egoist could provide is that we would be motivated to follow such rules not because we actually care about the interests of others but because it is in our interest to do so.

This last point is the crux of the matter for psychological egoism. If it is the case that human nature is such that it is exclusively self-interested, then it is not simply that we shouldn't act in the interest of others or that we sometimes act in both our own interest and the interest of others but rather that it is actually impossible to act in the interest of others at all. As a theory of motivation, psychological egoism denies that we are even partially motivated to act on behalf of others. It is simply impossible to be altruistic. Of course, others may in fact benefit from our actions, but their benefit is never the goal of such action, and we may actually desire the happiness of others but only as a means to our own satisfaction and never as an end in itself. In this way, psychological egoism is distinguished from, indeed inconsistent with, the weaker thesis of *psychological altruism*—the view that while self-interest is always present in motivation, we sometimes act with both our own interest and the interest of others in mind. So psychological egoism holds that there is only one motivation for human action; everything we do is explainable in terms of the singular conception that we only and always act to benefit ourselves.

Though psychological egoism paints a rather bleak picture of human nature, it nonetheless has a certain intuitive appeal. Many people tend to think that we always strive to do what is best for ourselves or satisfy our desires or do what we most want to do or do what makes us feel good in some sense. In his extensive analysis of psychological egoism, the philosopher Joel Feinberg identifies several *prima facie* reasons why some people find it a plausible theory of human motivation.[2] He suggests the following: i) every action one takes is motivated by his/her own desires, so we really just seek our own satisfaction; and if it is true that each and every action is so motivated, then we always act 'selfishly'; ii) when one gets what one wants—when one's desires are satisfied—one feels pleasure; from this we may conclude that pleasure is what we all really want; we may desire other things, but only as a means to attain pleasure; iii) we are often deceived into thinking that we have noble or virtuous motives, that we are altruistically inclined toward the benefit of others, when we are, in fact, really concerned with how we appear to others, or having a good feeling about ourselves, or congratulating ourselves; iv) moral education itself, understood as a system of rewards and punishment, proceeds by appealing to our natural desire to feel pleasure and avoid pain.[3]

Are any of these reasons, or is even the collection of them, sufficient to the task of constituting an argument that justifies one's believing that psychological egoism is actually true? Feinberg, along with many other philosophers, argues that psychological egoism is, in fact, demonstrably false. He suggests that none of these reasons provides empirical evidence for psychological egoism; they are really just general impressions some people have about human motivation. So, at the very least, there seems to be no scientific basis for the idea that we always act selfishly. It should be noted that some evolutionary biologists and contemporary neuroscientists might challenge this point. When viewed in the context of a scientific approach to human motivation, behavior is explainable, perhaps, simply in terms of our genetic make-up or on the basis of neural structures and mechanisms. Our genes may be "selfish," as Richard Dawkins has famously suggested, in that they evolve in terms of the satisfaction of those desires that specifically contribute to our survival. Some neuroscientists advocate a form of psychological egoism called *psychological hedonism*—the idea that experiencing pleasure is the sole motivation of human action—in arguing that the pleasure center of the brain is triggered when we attain the reward of having achieved the goal of an action. All this said, however, there are also scientists who claim to have empirical evidence to the contrary. Evolution may lead us to act more altruistically, since such action makes us more fit for living in society. Social psychologists might claim to have empirical evidence that empathetic feelings for others increase our capacity to have genuine altruistic motivation; neuroscientists may challenge the idea that the pleasure center in the brain is activated by successful completion of an action or the very idea that there is a pleasure center at all. Although the scientific community might be paying more attention to the fundamental thesis of psychological egoism, science as not yielded any conclusive results on the matter.[4]

In light of the fact that scientific investigation has not settled the issue, consider some of the more standard philosophical arguments against psychological egoism. First, it is simply a trivial claim that a person acts on his or her own desires, but it doesn't logically follow from this that one is always acting selfishly. Suppose John volunteers at a local soup kitchen on Saturday afternoons and assume that John is doing exactly what he desires to do. Though John's desire is, in some sense, satisfied by his performing an action that he wants to do, we still need to ask about the point of his action. What is the goal John hopes to achieve in performing the action? What is the real object of his desire? Is his desire satisfied simply by performing the action? It seems wrong, or odd at best, to think that John is satisfied solely in performing the action, since the action itself is directed toward others. John's own satisfaction, then, is connected to the actual benefit others receive from his doing what he does in the sense that what he really wants as a goal is that others benefit from his actions. The real object of John's desire is precisely that benefit.

From this it can be argued further that John is, in fact, being unselfish. John wants for others, in some way, to be made better off by his actions. This is just what it ordinarily means to say that someone is *unselfish*. Psychological egoism denies that there is any real semantic value, any meaning, to the expression *unselfish act*. But this is inconsistent with our ordinary linguistic usage and our everyday experience. In both instances, we distinguish between people who act selfishly and those who act unselfishly; and we do so precisely in terms of the goal of their desires. In caring about others, John demonstrates that he is not selfish.

Now a psychological egoist might respond by saying that we are simply deceived in this respect. We can always reinterpret the motive for any action along the lines of a psychologically egoistic conception of motives. John deceives himself into thinking that the object of his desire is the benefit of others when, in fact, he is really motivated by such things as the public recognition he might get for volunteering at the soup kitchen, or the good feeling he has in doing so, or—perhaps being religiously inclined—he believes that in performing such actions he will win favor with God and secure his eventual place in heaven. There are several responses we can make to the psychological egoist on this score. First, suppose John does feel good in helping others, it does not follow, as indicated above, that that is his point in acting. Such feelings or other self-beneficial rewards may be only collateral benefits and not primary goals or objects of his desire. In this way, John might legitimately protest that he is not acting selfishly. Second, this is a very weak defense of psychological egoism in that it does not establish the general truth of psychological egoism. It demonstrates only that psychological egoism could respond to specific counter-examples; it does not prove that we can never desire in non-egoistic ways. As James Rachels suggests, we can learn a general lesson about desire from all this. We desire or want all kinds of things—friends, fortune, fame, a vintage guitar, a nice house, etc.—and in such cases, it is not the feeling of satisfaction that we're after. It is the having of those things themselves that we want. Rachels says "it is the same with helping others; we may feel good by doing so, but it is that others are actually helped that matters."[5]

Finally, psychological egoism simply assumes that, in general, we are always and only motivated by desire; it ignores the possibility that there might be other motivations for acting. John might volunteer at the soup kitchen because he feels an obligation to help others when he can. In this respect John thinks of certain actions not primarily in terms of how they benefit anyone—himself or others—but fundamentally whether they are actions he simply ought to do because morality requires them. This last point raises the possibility that we may not always be motivated by desire or always do just what we want. There are many times in ordinary life when we act for some reason other than the satisfaction of our desires or doing what gives us pleasure or what makes us feel good. We often act out of a sense of fairness, and so might give up something we want so others may have a share. We might visit a sick relative, not because it's what we most want to do, but rather out a sense of obligation. We sometimes, with great discomfort, admit our wrongdoings to others and seek their forgiveness. We do things that are sometimes extremely uncomfortable maybe even painful, like going to the dentist or having a medical procedure; admittedly these may be in our best self-interest, but they could hardly be understood as objects of desire or sources of real pleasure.

The deepest difficulty with psychological egoism is that it has a general and unitary conception of human motivation, but as we have seen human motivation may be multi-varied and more complex than that conception can accommodate. The tortuous maneuvers psychological egoism must make in order to truncate all of human desire into its one dimensional model demonstrate its inadequacies. As a theory it fails to explain certain salient features of human experience—for instance, that the object of our desire is sometimes the good of others and not just our own feeling of satisfaction; it fails to explain meaningful distinctions in ordinary language—it cannot, for instance, account for the difference between "selfishness" and "unselfishness" and it fails to explain the important distinction between acting selfishly and acting in one's own best interest. Such distinctions are, in fact, meaningful and are more accurately descriptive of human experience than the claims made by psychological egoism.

Ethical Egoism

Though there are good reasons for believing that psychological egoism is false, those reasons do not demonstrate that ethical egoism is wrong. Recall that there is a difference between a descriptive theory and a normative theory; as a descriptive theory, psychological egoism makes a claim about how we are actually motivated to act; ethical egoism is a normative theory about what we should do. In so far as ethical egoism asserts that each individual should act in his/her own best interest, it recognizes that people sometimes act in ways counter to that principle. In general, when it is asserted that we ought to act in some way, it is implied that we are free to act in alternate ways.

For the psychological egoist, there really are no ways to act other than selfishly. If, in fact, it is impossible for persons to act altruistically (in the interest of others), then it just wouldn't make sense to say that we ought to act in the interest of others, or for that matter that we ought to act in any way. It appears then that if psychological egoism is true, then no moral theory, not even ethical egoism, can be true. Consequently, if ethical egoism were true, psychological egoism would be false, since the rightness or wrongness of actions is measured against our capacity to do the right thing in the face of real possible alternatives. In light of this, it is important to consider ethical egoism on its own and to evaluate its strength and weaknesses in terms of arguments different from those used to support or criticize psychological egoism.

Ethical egoism is the kind of moral theory that evaluates actions in terms of their capacity to bring about certain ends or goals. In this case, the goals or purposes are exclusively those that are in the agent's own best interest. So actions are morally right when they bring about what is in the best interest of the person performing the action, and actions are morally wrong when they fail to do so. From the perspective of ethical egoism, the very point of morality is to advance oneself by acting in ways that secure one's own advantage.

It is important to understand just how the ethical egoist means this. First, one's own advantage is the exclusive goal of moral action; even if along the way the interests of others happen to be advanced, that cannot be the goal of moral action. Second, what is in one's best interest is not necessarily the same thing as what gives one pleasure or makes one feel good. In this respect egoism is distinguished from self-directed form of hedonism (the view—considered later in this text—that pleasure and only pleasure is good). Third, acting in one's best interest is not the same as simply doing what one wants to do. People often want to do very dopey things; ethical egoism is not an invitation to act on such desires. Finally, one's own best interest counts more than the interest of others, even though egoism, in so far as it purports to be a universal moral theory, recommends that each individual acts in his or her own best interest.

Arguments in Favor of Ethical Egoism

As noted at the beginning of this chapter, it is a common conception to think that we should consider the interests of others when we act morally. Ethical egoism rejects this conception and denies that the interests of others need to be taken into account in our moral judgments. It is not enough simply to make this assertion. Ethical egoism must provide a justification for that claim. To serve that purpose, there are several arguments that could be offered in defense of ethical egoism. Here I am following in outline arguments that are presented and analyzed by Rachels in much finer detail.[6]

First, consider the following: Everyone, the whole of society, would be better off if each individual acted exclusively in his or her own best interest, so everyone ought to act in his or her own best interest. After all each of us knows what is best for ourselves and could, given our ignorance with respect to what others need, do more harm than good by efforts to act altruistically. Further, it may be unduly intrusive with respect to an individual's private understanding of his or her own needs to assume that it is morally good to act on their behalf. Moreover, we may demean others by presuming that they want our assistance, moral or otherwise. From this perspective, altruism would be self-defeating. If the argument does not show that altruism is downright inconsistent, it does at least call into question whether it is a morally superior position to act in the interest of others.

There is, however, an obvious flaw in this argument from the standpoint of ethical egoism itself. If the point of moral action is to secure one's own advantage, then what difference does it make whether everyone is better off or not? For ethical egoism, one's own best interest is the supreme moral value. Although the argument recognizes the value of acting out of self-interest, it justifies acting out of self-interest in terms of another, presumably higher, value—the general welfare of society. The general welfare of society however, is not something that the ethical egoist should consider in determining the goals of moral action. In the end, then, this argument appeals to the very kind of altruistic judgments that ethical egoism means to defeat.

A second line of approach in defending ethical egoism comes from the noted libertarian author and essayist, Ayn Rand. Rand, who in both her fiction and prose writing advocates a strong form of egoism, repudiates altruism, and elevates selfishness to the position of being the highest virtue. Consider the following lines from the character of Howard Roark, the radically individualistic architect and protagonist of Rand's novel *The Fountainhead*:

> The man who attempts to live for others is a dependent. He is a parasite in motive and makes parasites of those he serves. The relationship produces nothing but mutual corruption. It is impossible in concept. The nearest approach to it in reality—the man who lives to serve others— is the slave. If physical slavery is repulsive, how much more repulsive is the concept of servility

of the spirit? The conquered slave has a vestige of honor. He has the merit of having resisted and of considering his condition evil. But the man who enslaves himself voluntarily in the name of love is the basest of creatures. He degrades the dignity of man and he degrades the conception of love. But this is the essence of altruism.[7]

For Rand, altruism is not simply logically problematic, it is completely self-annihilating. It turns persons into parasites and dependents, and renders them incapable of acting for themselves.

Amidst the high rhetoric here, there is an underlying argument. Rand's argument could be structured this way:

1. Each individual has only one life and that life should be accorded ultimate value.
2. The ethics of pure altruism requires that an individual sacrifice his own life for others, and so denies that one's own life has ultimate value.
3. Only ethical egoism allows for one's own life to have ultimate value.
4. Therefore, altruism should be rejected and egoism embraced.

Rachels, in his analysis of this argument, makes several important observations. First, the argument really attacks a "straw man" in so far as it assumes that "pure altruism" is a real possibility. The idea that someone should or even could always act exclusively in the interest of others is preposterous on the face of it. Moreover, the argument sets up a false dichotomy between "pure altruism" and ethical egoism. Is the situation so black and white such that if one is not an egoist, then one is perforce a pure altruist? Isn't it possible to discern some middle ground? There is no logical inconsistency in claiming that both one's own interests and the interests of others count morally, and practical experience bears out the fact that it is possible to act for mutual benefit. There may indeed be occasions where interests conflict, but part of the task of moral philosophy and moral thinking in general is to try to resolve those conflicting situations.

A third, and perhaps more promising, defense of ethical egoism follows a neo-Hobbesian line of thought. Recall that Thomas Hobbes, a psychological egoist, argued that in our natural state our interests always conflict; in this condition, we may not survive very long. Hobbes also said that in society, the artifice we set up to ensure our own survival, we follow the rules of common sense morality, but we do so because it is in our best interest. It is to our own advantage to follow the rules of common sense morality (not harming others, being truthful, keeping our promises, etc.) and that is precisely why we follow such rules. It seems then that ethical egoism provides a defense for the very common sense notions of morality that it apparently calls into question. If we harm others, or lie to them, or break our promises, then others will treat us badly. The best way to ensure that others will treat us well is to treat them well and so it is in our best interest to act according to the rules of morality.

As promising as this may seem, there are two significant problems with the argument. First, it assumes that the rules of common sense morality and self-interest always coincide. But this is clearly not true. Sometimes it is to one's own benefit to break the rules. What should you do in that case? If you follow the rules, then you are not acting as an ethical egoist requires; in fact, in this circumstance you would be acting altruistically. If you break the rules and treat people badly, then that seems risky from the Hobbsian perspective upon which the argument is based to begin with. Moreover, not even ethical egoism, in so far as it purports to be a rational conception of morality, actively promotes doing evil. A second, and more serious, problem with this argument has to do with what counts as a reason for acting. Even if following the rules of common sense morality and self-interest always coincided, this would still not be enough to demonstrate that one's own benefit is the reason why we should perform certain actions. It may be one reason, but not the only or even the best reason for acting. Perhaps other people just deserve to be treated well.

Arguments against Ethical Egoism

The arguments discussed above all seem to fail in the attempt to provide a rational justification for the fundamental claims of ethical egoism, but the weakness of such arguments by itself does not constitute a reason for rejecting ethical egoism. This section considers arguments that are squarely directed against ethical egoism and attempt to provide a refutation of that theory. Here are several attempts to do just that.

Some have argued that ethical egoism actually endorses moral evil. Consider Rachels's example of a paramedic who injects patients with sterile water instead of morphine and then sells the morphine on the streets for a substantial profit. It is seemingly in the paramedic's interest to do so, yet the action is by all reasonable accounts morally evil.[8] So the argument goes: Some actions are in a person's interest but nonetheless morally wrong. We should not perform actions that are morally wrong. Egoism must therefore be false. On the face of it, the argument seems to work, but it is, in fact, problematic. First, it assumes a definition of moral evil that the egoist would not accept and leaves unexplained precisely how an action can be both self-interested and morally wrong. Moreover, an egoist could rightly question whether it is actually in one's best interest to engage in such actions.

Another line of approach is to focus on certain logical problems inherent in theory of ethical egoism. Such issues have to do with ethical egoism's ability: 1) to settle moral conflicts; 2) to provide sound moral advice, and 3) to reach consistent conclusions. Let's consider each of these problems in turn.

Conflicts of interest occur all the time, and assuming that morality is defined in terms of self-interest, such conflicts are moral conflicts. Egoism, in so far as it relies exclusively on self-interest to define the moral, can appeal to no other independent standard that can be employed to settle conflicts. Any moral theory should provide the means for settling disputes. Therefore, egoism fails as a moral theory. This argument does not definitively defeat ethical egoism, in that the egoist could simply reject the idea that moral theories are designed to resolve conflict. The moral life, like other aspects of life, is a competition. If interests conflict, absent any impartial standard that can be used to resolve the conflict, one will simply win out over the other.

A variant of the conflict argument extends the analysis to a consideration of the idea of giving moral advice. The argument attempts to show that ethical egoism fails because it cannot consistently maintain the universality of its fundamental principle that everyone should act in his or her own best interest. Suppose you come to me for moral advice and in the course of our conversation, I realize that what would be best for you directly conflicts with what is best for me. How should I advise you? If I advise you to be an egoist and act for your own self-interest, I may be harming myself. But, according to ethical egoism, it is wrong for me to do anything that is not in my best interest. So seemingly I should then advise you to do what I know is not in your best interest. However, in doing so, I am advising you to act in a non-egoistic way. Put more strongly: I should advise you to do what is in my best interest, even though it conflicts with your best interest; in doing so, I would be advising you to act altruistically. Isn't there an inconsistency in that? An ethical egoist could respond, however, that there really is no formal contradiction here. I could act in my own best interest and you could still act in yours, irrespective of whatever advice I might give. Further, ethical egoism does not, in this instance, impose any moral obligation on me to advise you one way or another.

There may be a more straightforward logical approach to take in an effort to demonstrate the inherent inconsistency in ethical egoism. Kurt Baier, in his highly influential work *The Moral Point of View*, constructs an argument designed to show that ethical egoism leads to contradictory conclusions (that the same action is both right and wrong) and so should, on that basis, be rejected as an adequate moral theory. His argument is based on the general view that self-interest and morality are frequently opposed to each other. He writes that "morality often requires us to refrain from doing what self-interest recommends or to do what self-interest forbids."[9] Though it is often reasonable to act on the basis of self-interest, it does not follow that self-interest and morality are the same thing. Baier attempts to demonstrate this by showing the logical inconsistency of egoism. He asks us to imagine two persons running for president of a country; each has an interest in winning and each has an interest in thwarting the other's efforts. Let's call them Ms. Liberal (L) and Mr. Conservative (C) and let's use Baier's extreme example—that the best way to thwart the other is to liquidate that person. So it is in Ms. L's interest to liquidate Mr. C and on that basis she has a moral duty to liquidate Mr. C. At the same time, Mr. C has an interest in staying alive and so has a moral duty to prevent Ms. L from liquidating him. Here's the difficulty as Baier sees it: Based on the assumption that ethical egoism is true, Mr. C's effort to prevent Ms. L from liquidating him is both right and wrong. It is right because, obviously, it is Mr. C's best interest, but it is wrong because it is not right for Mr. C to prevent Ms. L from doing her moral (ethically egoistic) duty. Here's the logical point: If we assume the truth of ethical egoism, then one action turns out to be both right and wrong, but that's a contradiction, and therefore ethical egoism must be false.[10]

Perhaps the problem with this argument is already obvious. As Rachels notes, the contradiction derives not from the definition of ethical egoism alone but from that definition along with the added notion that *it is wrong to prevent someone from doing his or her duty.*[11] There is no reason, however, why an ethical egoist must accept that prohibition. If it's in your best interest to prevent someone from performing any action, then from the standpoint of ethical egoism, it would be right to do so. It's only wrong to prevent another from acting if it runs counter to your interest in doing so. Isn't that just what egoism says?

The persistent efforts to refute ethical egoism on the basis that it is logically inconsistent seem to arrive at dead ends. A more productive approach may be to consider certain substantive claims and see how egoism stacks up against them. Here we will consider two such arguments—James Rachels's argument that egoism is unacceptably arbitrary and an argument that self-interest alone cannot qualify as a reason for acting morally.

Rachels's argument is based on his acceptance of a moral principle he calls the *principle of equal treatment*. The principle states that we should treat people equally unless there is some relevant factual difference that warrants a difference in treatment. There may indeed be many such factual differences—disabilities, talents, physical ability, etc.—that justify treating people differently in certain circumstances. There are other differences, however, that are factual but which nonetheless do not warrant any differential moral treatment. Consider the case of racism. Racism is arbitrary or unduly discriminatory because there are no morally relevant differences between the races that would justify treating members of one group differently. [12]

Rachels argues analogously that ethical egoism involves a similar type of arbitrary discrimination. Ethical egoism divides the world into two groups—me and everyone else—and claims that the interests of one group (me) count more than the interests of the other group (everyone else). But what makes oneself so special? Do you have unique needs, a richer capacity to enjoy life, some special ability, etc. that warrants according greater moral value to yourself than to everyone else? Without a clear answer to such questions, ethical egoism is an arbitrary doctrine in much the same way that racism is arbitrary. There is no basis on which to assign greater moral value to one's own interest than to anyone else's. From the moral point of view, we ought to treat people equally because our interests are similar, and we ought to factor the interests of others along with self-interest into our moral judgments. Rachels takes this to be a refutation of ethical egoism, but whether the argument is that strong depends on the acceptance or rejection of the principle of equal treatment.

Finally, consider an argument about what qualifies as a moral reason. [13] The argument is that self-interest cannot qualify as a reason for acting morally, since reasons for moral action belong to no one in particular. How might this work? Consider the following simple example. It's a very hot day and I'm walking down an avenue in Manhattan, and I have very strong desire for a cool drink and it is in my interest, of course, to stay sufficiently hydrated. Out of the corner of my eye, I spot a man at an outdoor café table. His bottle of sparkling water is easily within my grasp and he's involved in rapt conversation with his companion, so he likely wouldn't immediately notice if I grabbed the bottle and drank from it. So why shouldn't I take the bottle and drink from it? Before we answer, let's reverse the situation. Now I'm at the table and a hot, thirsty walker takes my drink. I certainly wouldn't like it, but more than this I would resent it precisely because I think that person has a reason not to treat me so badly. It is the same reason I have for objecting to the ill treatment and others ought to recognize that reason. This is a fanciful way of asking, "How would you like it if somebody did that to you?" Now back to the original scenario—I'm on the street contemplating taking the water, but I consider that I would resent it if someone did that to me and refrain from doing so. Now my reason for not taking the water is the same reason why the man at the table objects to having his water taken.

The point of this example is to show that a reason for acting morally can be anybody's reason and that my reason is just that kind of reason, one that any moral-thinking person could use. Thomas Nagel calls this the "How would you like it?" argument. Nagel puts it this way:

> . . . if you admit that you would *resent* it if someone else did to you what you are now doing to him, you are admitting that you think he would have a reason not to do it to you. And if you admit that, you have to consider what that reason is. It couldn't be just that it's *you* that he's hurting, of all the people in the world. . . . There's nothing so special about you. Whatever the reason is, it's a reason he would have against hurting anyone in the same way. And it's a reason anyone else would have too, in a similar situation, against hurting you or anyone else.[14]

Just as in Rachels's equal treatment argument, this argument gives no special prominence to one's own self-interest. Beyond this, the argument may demonstrate the deepest flaw in ethical egoism;

namely, that it divorces one's so-called reasons for acting from the objective context within which the idea of giving reasons makes sense at all and encourages a kind of moral isolationism. None of this is to suggest that we embrace pure altruism, but it is meant to suggest that in the moral world, we just can't go it alone.

ENDNOTES

1. Thomas Hobbes, *Leviathan*, Chapter XIII.

2. Joel Feinberg, "Psychological Egoism" reprinted in *Ethical Theory: An Anthology*, Second Edition edited by Russ Shafer-Landau. (John Wiley & Sons, Inc., 2013), pp. 167–177.

3. Feinberg, p. 168.

4. For a brief summary of these issues see the entry on "Psychological Egoism" by Joshua May in the *Internet Encyclopedia of Philosophy* (http://www.iep.utm.edu/psychego/#SH2a).

5. Stuart Rachels, *The Elements of Moral Philosophy* Eight Edition (McGraw Hill, 2015), pp. 70–71.

6. Rachels, pp. 71–76.

7. Ayn Rand, *The Fountainhead* (1943).

8. Rachels, pp. 76–77.

9. Kurt Baier, *The Moral Point of View: A Rational Basis of Ethics* Abridged Edition (Random House, 1965), p. 93.

10. Baier, pp. 95-96. See also Rachels's discussion of Baier's argument in *The Elements of Moral Philosophy*, pp. 77–78.

11. Rachels, p. 78.

12. Rachels, pp. 79–81.

13. This argument is based on ideas from Thomas Nagel. Nagel argues that a moral reason can be objective in that it is not just my reason, but a reason that anyone can use. See especially chapter 7 on right and wrong in his *What Does It All Mean* (Oxford University Press, 1987). Here I apply

this idea in an argument specifically directed against ethical egoism.

14. Nagel, *What Does It All Mean*, pp. 65–66.

STUDY QUESTIONS

1. Distinguish between *psychological egoism* and *ethical egoism*.

2. Explain Hobbes's view of human nature. In what sense is Hobbes a psychological egoist?

3. What is *altruism*? Explain why psychological egoism claims that altruism is impossible.

4. What are some reasons why people might find psychological egoism a plausible theory of human motivation? What is psychological egoism's strategy for reinterpreting motives?

5. Identify and explain three arguments in favor of ethical egoism.

6. How might it be argued that ethical egoism is logically inconsistent?

7. What is Rachels's *principle of equal treatment*? How does Rachels employ the principle in his argument against ethical egoism?

8. How could the concept of a moral reason be used in an argument against ethical egoism?

QUESTIONS FOR REFLECTION

1. Consider the difference between acting selfishly and acting out of self-interest. Do you think that the distinction could be used to justify ethical egoism? Why or why not?

2. Evaluate Ayn Rand's argument in favor of ethical egoism. Is selfishness a virtue? Do you agree or disagree with Rand's viewpoint?

3. It is a common moral view to think that we should consider how our actions affect others. Does acting for the benefit of others necessarily imply that we can't also act in our own interest? Explain.

4. Evaluate Rachels's argument against egoism. Do you think it constitutes a "refutation" of ethical egoism? Why or why not?

5. Does the *"How would you like it?"* argument defeat ethical egoism?

SUGGESTIONS FOR FURTHER READING

Broad, C. D. *Five Types of Ethical Theory*. London: Kegan Paul, Trench, Trubner & Co. Ltd., 1930. (Reprinted by Routledge, 2000).

Broad, C. D. "Egoism as a Theory of Human Motives." *The Hibbert Journal* Vol. 48, 1950.

Darwall, Stephen. "Egoism and Morality" in Desmond M. Clarke & Catherine Wilson (eds.), *The Oxford Handbook of Philosophy in Early Modern Europe*. Oxford: Oxford University Press, 2011.

Dawkins, Richard. *The Selfish Gene*. 30th anniversary edition with new introduction, New York: Oxford University Press, 2006.

Nagel, Thomas. *The Possibility of Altruism*. Oxford: Clarendon Press, 1970.

Rand, Ayn. *Virtue of Selfishness*. New York: Signet, 1964.

Williams, Bernard. "Egoism and Altruism." Ch. 15 in *Problems of the Self: Philosophical Papers 1956–1972*. Cambridege, UK: Cambridge University Press, 1973.

chapter 3

Value

One of the most challenging questions in moral philosophy is: What is the good life? What makes the question so difficult to negotiate is that the answer depends on determining just what things are valuable to desire, to pursue, and to have. The complexity in this is immediately apparent when we consider the myriad desires persons have and the multitude of things we believe have some sort of value in our lives. We have interests and desires and tend to think that whatever satisfies those is good for us in that it makes a positive difference to us. We believe that some things have negative value or are bad for us; they make a difference to us, but not in a positive way. We also tend to think that something has positive value for us when it aids in our getting something else. For instance, going to college is good because it is a way to earn a degree, having a degree is a means to a good job, having a good job leads to making money, having money is a way to get other things—a nice car, a home theatre, a trip to Italy, membership in an upscale golf club, and so on. But is everything we call good or valuable good in this sense? Is everything good only in so far as it delivers something else that makes a positive difference to us? Can we persist in the line of thinking that views all goods as means to something else? Wouldn't we arrive at a stopping place? Why might you want the nice car, the home theatre, the trip to Italy, the golf club membership? A typical answer goes something like this: It would make me happy to have and do those things.

Now consider: Does it make sense, in this case, to ask why do you want to be happy? Here we may have reached the end of the line in our questioning, not because happiness itself isn't good, but precisely because it is good, but in a special way—good not as means to something else, but good as an end in itself, as that which might have been the ultimate goal all along. Is there an ultimate good for us? Is that good happiness or something else? If there is something that is of ultimate value for us, then it must matter with respect to what it means to lead a good life. The question of what, if anything, has ultimate value for us involves a nexus of concerns about having certain kinds of conscious states, performing actions, the evaluation of desires and preferences, what sorts of things are worth wanting, the pursuit of objectively determinable goods, and the communal context in which we seek satisfaction and pursue our goals. In fine, the idea of value is central to our understanding of what it means to live a life that is worth living.

The idea of the good life is, of course, an age-old problem, but there are contemporary exigencies that make it perhaps more pressing now than ever that we treat the problem with a renewed sense of importance. Peter Singer, the contemporary moral philosopher, writes that there is a "need to challenge the dominance of the assumption that the good life requires ever-rising standards of moral material affluence" as there seems to be no evidence that material wealth makes persons happier. In addition, he suggests that the current affluent lifestyle of many persons strains our planet's resources and limits its capacity to accommodate all the waste such a lifestyle produces.[1] If one thinks of the good life as inextricably connected to our being global citizens, then this view might appear especially significant. Or consider a different line of thought, one more closely associated with the idea that the good life requires living a life of self-determination, relatively free from external constraints and reasonably free to live as one chooses without fear of harm or annihilation. Many people in the contemporary world live under the oppression of unjust political power or the fear of fanaticism and are unable to live their lives as they desire. If one thinks that oppression, fanaticism, terror, and torture threaten the very possibility of achieving good ends, then that may be the prompt for deeper reflection and a revived sense of urgency about the importance of value and goodness in human life. The point here is not that we must decide which of these views is correct, but rather that the problem of the good life is not merely an abstract consideration. The concrete realities of life may alter our conception of what counts as good but not our idea that the good matters at all.

The question here is really one about means to ends. If we can identify the good, then we should be able to figure out how best to achieve it. There are two different senses of the term good then that are applicable here. Something can be good as a means to an end, or something can be good as an end or that which we hope to achieve. That which is good as a means is called an *instrumental good*. Think again about the examples above. We value money, for instance. It is a good for us, but it is not an end in itself. We use it for getting other things that we might deem valuable. That which is good in itself is called an *intrinsic good*. An intrinsic good is something that is worth having on its own; we don't use it for something else the way we use money to purchase things. Instead the intrinsic good is understood as that which is valuable to have for no other purpose than that it is good for us. This is an important distinction because it implies that there must be something that constitutes an ultimate good; that is, something is good as a means to an end only if the end is something that is itself good. If there was no good or desirable end, then it wouldn't make sense to speak of something good as means to that end. To say otherwise would involve us in an infinite regress: A is good because it is a means to B; B is good because it is a means to C; C is good because it is a means to D; and so on *ad infinitum*. So there needs to be a stopping place, without which there would be an infinite set of goods with no distinct reason as to why any of them are good at all. So the problem of the good is not fundamentally about this or that thing in a series of goods, but about what gives meaning to the whole series itself. We can say it's about what makes it all worthwhile.

Though we speak of something's being intrinsically good or having value in and of itself, it is nonetheless the case that even that which is good in itself has worth *for* us. Something has value or worth *for* us because we are conscious creatures. Consciousness is the condition for experiencing the good and being aware of its worth. Desire itself is a conscious state that directs us toward that which we find desirable. In this regard, there is nothing that is good for a rock or any inanimate object. But there are many living things that also lack consciousness. Take a plant, for instance. We do often say that it is good for a houseplant to have the proper amount of water and light in order to thrive. All we really mean here is that the plant has a biological need for sufficient water and light if it is to continue to survive; it makes no sense to say that the plant "desires" water and light, that it "finds" water and light valuable, or that it "judges" its life worthwhile if it has those things. Matters get more complicated when we think of animals, especially higher order animals that do display a degree of consciousness, which may minimally require that we treat them with a certain measure of moral respect, if not accord them some capacity to pursue desired ends. The general point here is that the good is only good for a thing if that thing has the ability to experience it.

It is one thing, however, to say that consciousness is the condition for something being good for us and quite another to say that the good itself is a state of consciousness; pleasure, for instance. Many philosophers argue that only states of consciousness—pleasant feelings or pleasurable sensations perhaps—can qualify as intrinsically good. Others argue that it is not the state of consciousness itself that matters but rather suggest that the kind of object that is desired is what matters to us. One way of considering this difference is to ask the following question: Is the good simply having certain experiences or is it experiencing things of a certain sort and in a certain way? There is a difference, for instance, in being able to play the guitar and having a pleasant experience in doing so. Do we only want to feel good or do we desire to do things and perform actions? Is the good realized in the experience alone or in the performance or ability itself? Such questions lead us squarely to a consideration of competing philosophical theories about the nature of the good.

Hedonism

One particularly enduring conception of the good is that given in a theory called hedonism. Hedonism is rooted in a view of human nature and human psychology that says we are fundamentally motivated to experience pleasure and avoid pain. Under this view, pleasure is desired as an end and pain is considered to be that which is undesirable. The hedonist argues that:

1. Something is good if and only if it is desirable as an end in itself.
2. Only pleasure is desirable as an end in itself.
3. Therefore, only pleasure is good.

Hedonism relies on the distinction drawn above between intrinsic and instrumental goods, and makes two fundamental claims: 1) all pleasure is intrinsically good and 2) only pleasure is intrinsically good. Of course, there are many things that are instrumentally good insofar as they bring about pleasure. For example, liberty is an instrumental good as a means to experiencing more and greater pleasure. It might even be the case that although pain is in and of itself something undesirable, it can be instrumental for experiencing pleasure. Think of the physical pain you may experience as the result of a vigorous workout and the pleasure felt as a result of an improved bodily condition. It is the pleasure that we are ultimately after and we are perhaps even willing to endure a bit of pain to get there.

Now we can understand hedonism more fully. The hedonist believes that the only thing that is desirable in itself is pleasure. Pleasure is the only thing that we desire for its own sake, and not because it leads to something else that is desirable. In saying that pleasure is the only thing that is desirable in itself, hedonism is not saying that one's own pleasure counts more than anyone else's experience. Hedonism is not the same thing as egoism. In contrast to egoism, hedonists claim that anyone's pleasure is good. It doesn't matter whether it's mine or yours; pleasure, all pleasure, is good.

This form of hedonism serves as the foundation for the development of the normative ethical theory called *utilitarianism.* Utilitarianism is a type of theory called *consequentialism.* Consequentialism is the idea that the rightness or wrongness of an action is determined by the consequences, good or bad respectively, of the action. The distinguishing feature of utilitarianism is that it holds that we should perform those actions which maximize good consequences, not just for ourselves but ideally for all those who are affected by the action; that is, we should strive to bring about "the greatest good for the greatest number."

The early utilitarian thinkers Jeremy Bentham (1748–1832) and John Stuart Mill (1806–1873) were hedonists in that they identified pleasure as the greatest good. They understood the utility of an action as its tendency to increase pleasure and diminish pain. Under this view, an action has positive utility if brings about more pleasure than pain and negative utility if it does the opposite. Actions thus have instrumental value in that they are the means for securing the good. Utilitarianism views morality as an effort to ensure that as many as possible are able to experience the good to some extent or other. The next chapter focuses on utilitarianism as a normative moral theory; here the emphasis is on the idea of the good itself as that which motivates moral action.

Though both Bentham and Mill are hedonists, their views differ in significant ways, specifically with respect to both the sources of pleasure and kinds of pleasures. The Benthamite view is a *quantitative* form of hedonism. For Bentham, all pleasures are equal as being goods in themselves; pleasures differ only in amount or degrees of magnitude. There is no difference among the sources of pleasure as they are evaluated solely in terms of their capacity to produce the greatest amount of pleasure. There would be no difference between playing a simple game and listening to music or reading poetry. Bentham writes:

. . . the value they possess is exactly in proportion to the pleasure they yield. . . . Prejudice apart, the game of push-pin is of equal value with the arts and sciences of music and poetry. If the game of push-pin furnish more pleasure, it is more valuable than either. Everybody can play at push-pin: poetry and music are relished only by a few. . . . If poetry and music deserve to be preferred before a game of push-pin, it must be because they are *calculated* [my emphasis] to gratify those individuals who are most difficult to be pleased.[2]

The idea of calculated gratification is emphasized here because Bentham designed a set of quasi-mathematical criteria—the hedonistic calculus, as it is often called—to measure magnitudes of and relationships among pleasurable states as well as the tendency of acts to produce those states. Bentham considered pleasure or pain as a straightforward bodily sensation and believed that such a sensation could be measured according to the following standards: 1) *intensity*, 2) *duration*, 3) *certainty*, 4) *propinquity*, 5) *fecundity*, 6) *purity*, and 7) *extent*.

The *intensity* of a pleasure or pain is simply how strong the sensation is. It is common these days to see on your doctor's wall a "pain chart" with a scale of 0–10, ranging from no pain sensation to the most intense pain. The doctor asks where on the scale you would put your pain; in identifying a place on the scale, you give your pain a numerical value. *Duration* is the measurement of how long the sensation persists. Pleasure may be highly intense, but fleeting or it may be relatively mild, but long-lasting. As a side note: Bentham seems to have in mind measuring pleasure or pain sensations in terms of standard units of time measurement—minutes, hours, etc. He doesn't factor in the subjective attitudes we have in relation to pleasure and pain that make time feel different. Einstein's famous description of relativity works to illustrate what this means: "Put your hand on a hot stove for a minute, and it seems like an hour. Sit with a pretty girl for an hour, and it seems like a minute." It would be much more difficult, if not impossible, to measure pleasure/pain sensations if that psychological dimension were considered. By *certainty* is meant the likelihood that a pleasure will or will not occur. For instance, we learn through experience what sorts of actions yield which sensations. On that basis we could assign a value to the probability that a pleasurable sensation will occur. *Propinquity* (nearness) is also determined by units of time measurement, how near or how remote is the sensation from the action that produces it. Bentham suggests that these four criteria apply to a pain or pleasure sensation proper. *Fecundity* and *purity* are technically not properties of pleasure or pain but rather are ways to determine the tendency of actions to produce those sensations. *Fecundity* is the term used to describe the probability that a sensation will be followed by sensations of the same sort; *purity* is the probability that a sensation will not be followed by its opposite. *Extent* has to do with the distribution of pleasure or pain among those affected by an action.

Bentham uses his hedonistic calculus not simply for the purpose of quantifying pleasure, but also as what he took to be a purely objective approach to determining morally right actions. The chapter on utilitarianism examines how these criteria could be applied in such a way that we can compare possible courses of actions and outcomes in terms of placing on them a numerical value. Whether that works as a decision procedure for choosing moral actions is the basis for serious criticisms of the Benthamite form of hedonistic utilitarianism.

Though inspired by Bentham's sense that right action is determined by its consequences and that the purpose of morality is to bring about the greatest good for the greatest number, John Stuart Mill had a different understanding of hedonism. Like his predecessor, Mill embraced psychological hedonism, that conception of human nature that says we are constituted so as to desire pleasure and avoid pain, and he adopted the fundamental principles of hedonism; namely, that pleasure is intrinsically good and only pleasure is intrinsically good. But Mill rejected the idea that all pleasures are equal and that they differ only in degrees of magnitude; that is, Mill rejected the quantitative form of hedonism.

Instead, he argued that pleasures differ in terms of quality. Mill writes:

> It is quite compatible with the principle of utility to recognize the fact that some kinds of pleasure are more desirable and more valuable than others. It would be absurd that, while, in estimating all other things, quality is considered as well as quantity, the estimation of pleasures should be supposed to depend on quantity alone.[3]

So when we evaluate pleasure, we should consider the kind of pleasure that it is. Here Mill is responding to a common objection to Bentham's approach that hedonism amounts to nothing more than just crass pleasure-seeking.

Mill makes a distinction between *higher* and *lower* pleasures. The lower pleasures are shared by persons and animals, but a person's satisfaction in life requires more than just having pleasurable bodily sensations, however intense or long-lasting these might be. The experience of a higher quality of pleasure employs the use of the higher faculties. The quality of pleasure that satisfies a human is different from that which satisfies an animal. People are capable of more than animals, so it takes more to make a person happy. It doesn't take much, for instance, to satisfy a pig—some mud to roll in, some slop to eat, and the company of other pigs might be all it takes. The enjoyment quotient of a pig is considerably lower than that of a person, particularly in light of the fact that a person may be satisfied in terms of the lower pleasures and yet still feel unfilled. No reasonable person, if given the choice, would consent to leading the life of an animal, even if his or her desire for higher pleasures were unsatisfied. Still some people pursue bodily pleasures at the expense of higher intellectual or emotional ones. The pleasure one experiences from eating chocolate is, no doubt, good but is, in the Millean sense, lower than the intellectual pleasure one might experience, say, from solving a complex problem in mathematics. The pleasure of orgasm is intense, but the experience of it may be richly enhanced by a strong emotional affection felt between sexual partners. About this, Mill famously said: "It is better to be a human being dissatisfied than a pig satisfied; better to be Socrates dissatisfied than a fool satisfied. And if the fool or the pig are of a different opinion, it is because they only know their side of the question."

This last point is crucial. If we experience both kinds of pleasures—the lower and the higher ones—we will continue to pursue the higher ones, not at the expense of satisfying our animal desires, as these are not at odds with our higher capacities, but because they are more commensurate with our faculties and abilities. Moreover, Mill's qualitative approach demonstrates that hedonism is more than a theory about gratifying our brute animal urges. It avoids some of the pitfalls of quantitative hedonism and understands the idea of pleasure in the context of the salient human desire to lead a flourishing life and it views persons as particularly good judges of what it might take to achieve that end.

Nonetheless, Mill's emphasis on the idea that pleasure is the only intrinsic good is problematic. If there is a distinction between higher and lower pleasures and the higher ones are better for us, then it seems that there must be a criterion for making that judgment. And if there is a standard whereby we can distinguish some pleasures as "better" than others, then it follows that there must be something other than pleasure that counts as good. More precisely, if it is better to be Socrates dissatisfied than a fool satisfied, then the experience of pleasure is not all that matters. We often judge some experiences, even those that are less pleasurable than others, as being better for us. In order to make such a judgment at all requires employing a criterion of evaluation other than the feeling of pleasure itself. This apparent inconsistency in qualitative hedonism calls into question at least one of the fundamental theses of hedonism; namely, that pleasure is the only thing that is intrinsically good. It may be that, despite his insistence on the hedonistic conception of the good, Mill supplies the ground for further criticism of hedonism. We turn now to some criticisms of hedonism and a consideration of several alternate conceptions of the good.

Some Criticisms of Hedonism

Hedonism holds a *monistic* view of the good. This means that there is only one thing that is good in itself. There is, however, no inconsistency in holding that there are things other than pleasure that could qualify as intrinsically good. One could be *pluralistic* with respect to value and suggest that there are many such things—for example, talent, knowledge, beauty, liberty, friendship, happiness. A value *pluralist* may or may not include pleasure in the mix. Either way such a view is not hedonism as it violates one or both of the fundamental theses of hedonism. If one holds that there are many intrinsic goods and pleasure is among them, then she is not a hedonist in that she denies that pleasure is the only intrinsic good. If another holds that there are many intrinsic goods and pleasure is not among them, then he is not a hedonist in that he denies that pleasure is intrinsically good at all. Think again of Finnis's set of basic human goods (discussed in the chapter on moral objectivism)—life, knowledge, play, aesthetic experience, friendship, practical reasonableness, and religion. Each of these is a fundamental good, an intrinsic value, necessary for the good life. Achieving such ends may be accompanied by a feeling of pleasure or satisfaction, but according to Finnis, for instance, their goodness does not rely on that satisfaction; just having them is sufficient. For example, what we want and should pursue is not the satisfaction that might accompany knowledge, though that wouldn't be bad; what we want primarily is knowledge itself.

Now one need not, of course, be a hedonist to reject this idea of the good. That is to say, it may be the case that desire satisfaction must figure in any theory of what counts as good for us, but desire satisfaction is not necessarily construed in terms of pleasure. Suppose, for instance, a person desires to live the life of an ascetic, a self-disciplined life free of pleasurable indulgences. For whatever reasons, this person desires a life of spiritual contemplation and quietude without the distractions of pleasure. It is not the feeling of pleasure that is desired but the contemplation and quietude themselves. Suppose further that the person attains those ends and feels content in having achieved the desired life. Wouldn't we want to say that such a person's life is better for having realized his or her desired ends? The hedonist would think that such a life fails to be better because it lacks the requisite pleasure experiences. A *desire satisfaction theorist*, in contrast to the hedonist, says that the good life is achieved by attaining what we want, even if what we want is not the experience or feeling of pleasure.

There is an obvious problem, however, with saying that the good life is simply getting what you want. Isn't it the case that people are not always good judges and have desires for things that are counterproductive for a good life? Think of the compulsive gambler who desires the thrill of the bet, but who loses his life savings in the process, or the masochist whose desire to be miserable is fulfilled, or the character of Ebenezer Scrooge whose miserly sensibility and desire for money nearly destroys his capacity for even the most ordinary forms of human relationship. In such cases, we judge those lives as precisely the sorts which fail to be made better in virtue of the satisfaction of desire alone. If it is possible to have your desires satisfied and still not have attained a better life, then the desire satisfaction theory fails to provide an adequate conception of what constitutes the good life.

Though non-hedonistic in nature, this argument is structurally similar to Mill's argument against the quantitative form of hedonism. As Mill distinguished between higher and lower pleasures, so here we might distinguish between kinds of desires—those that are more or less conducive to leading a flourishing human life. But in saying this much, it seems necessary that there be a standard for evaluating desires that is something other than the satisfaction of desires itself. We ought to be able to determine which ends are most desirable in the sense that they are most fitting for us as persons.

In this respect, we might think not so much of the mere satisfaction of desires but rather about what it is that gives us fulfilment in life. Two things, both of which have to do with how our desires map on to the world, seem especially important when we consider the conditions of that fulfilment. First, it's not just pleasant experiences or the feeling of being satisfied that matters for fulfilment, it's that the circumstances in the world are such that we can actually do those things that yield the feeling of being satisfied. Second, fulfilment seemingly requires not just the satisfaction of desires but that the satisfaction succeeds in that it accurately reflects the way the world is. Here are two examples from James Rachels[4] to illustrate these points:

1. *A promising young pianist's hands are injured in an automobile accident so that she can no longer play.* Why is this bad for her? Hedonism would say it is bad because it causes her unpleasant feelings. She will feel frustrated and upset whenever she thinks of what might have been and *that* is her misfortune. But doesn't this type of reasoning explain things the wrong way around? It is not as though, by feeling unhappy, she has made an otherwise neutral situation into a bad one. On the contrary, her unhappiness is a rational response to a situation that *is* unfortunate. She could have had a career as a concert pianist, and now she cannot. That is the tragedy. We could not eliminate the tragedy just by getting her to cheer up, that is, by getting her to have pleasant feelings.

2. *You think someone is your friend, but he ridicules you behind your back.* No one tells you, so you never know. Is this unfortunate for you? Hedonism would have to say no because you are never caused any unhappiness. Is something bad still going on?

The first example illustrates the fact that we are not simply content in having good feelings, precisely because it is not simply the feelings that we value. In this case, the pianist values the talent and her unhappiness results from the fact that the circumstances in the world are such that she can longer perform actions that exemplify that talent. The second case illustrates the fact that although good feelings are present, it would still be possible for one's life to be going badly, even if one were unaware of the actual circumstances that obtain in the world. True enough that desires aren't claims about the world, but shouldn't it matter whether the feelings we have in some way reflect the way the world is? Wouldn't the satisfaction you feel in believing that one is your friend when in fact that person undermines the friendship behind your back be illusory in some sense? If so, then it seems that one's fulfillment in life depends not solely on how one feels but, more fundamentally, on how one's feelings succeed in mapping on to the world.

A particularly powerful argument against hedonism comes from the philosopher Robert Nozick. The argument is put forward in the form of a thought-experiment designed to show that we value something other than pleasure and that more things matter to us than just our own internal conscious states. Nozick asks that we imagine an experience machine that would, if we hooked up to it, enable to us to feel anything we desired. Here's how the thought-experiment goes:

> Suppose there were an experience machine that would give you any experience you desired. Superduper neuropsychologists could stimulate your brain so that you would think and feel you were writing a great novel, or making a friend, or reading an interesting book. All the time you would be floating in a tank with electrodes attached to your brain. Should you plug into this machine for life, preprogramming your life's experiences? If you are worried about missing out on desirable experiences, we can suppose that business enterprises have researched thoroughly the lives of many others. You can pick and choose from their large library or smorgasbord of such experiences, selecting your life's experiences for, say, the next two years. After two years have passed, you will have ten minutes or ten hours out of the tank, to select the experiences of your *next* two years. Of course, while in the tank you won't know that you're there; you'll think it's all actually happening. Others can also plug in to have the experiences

they want, so there's no need to stay unplugged to serve them. (Ignore problems such as who will service the machines if everyone plugs in.) Would you plug in?"[5]

From a straightforward hedonistic perspective, we should just want to plug into such a machine. After all it's the feeling that counts. Upon further consideration, however, we might come to realize that there are other things that are important to us and wish not to plug into the machine because doing so would prevent us from achieving what really matters. Nozick identifies three such things: 1) we actually want to do certain things; 2) we want to be certain kinds of persons; and 3) we don't want to be limited to an artificial, man-made reality. Take each of these in turn.

1) We actually want to do certain things. Consider again the example of the piano player who loses the use of her hands in a tragic accident. Even if she imagined that she could play the piano, the fact remains that she no longer can. So what is it that she really wants—to feel like she's playing the piano or to be able to play the piano? No amount of time spent hooked up to the experience machine changes the fact that she can no longer perform those actions associated with her talents and her life is made worse off for that reason. The difference between feeling from the inside that one is doing something and actually doing it must make a difference in terms of what makes one's life go better.

2) We want to be certain kinds of persons. If a person were hooked up to the experience machine, he or she would exhibit no signs of personhood, but would be merely a protoplasmic blob. Again the mere experience of being a certain kind of person is distinct from actually being a certain kind of person. Suppose you believe that your life is made better by being a generous person. If your life is to be made better by your being generous, then it isn't sufficient that you just feel as if you have that character trait; one's generosity is manifest in generous acts. Being a certain kind of person actually requires doing certain things—giving to charity, taking care of your children, showing gratitude, etc. While attached to

the machine, one is quite literally doing nothing and thus really being no kind of person. Nozick suggests that attachment to the machine is a kind of self-annihilation.

3) We don't want to be limited to an artificial reality; we want real attachments to the world and to other people. The world of the experience machine is substantively no different than a hallucinatory world. As we maneuver through the actual world and encounter real people, we modify our judgments, re-organize our desires, and adjust our projects and plans accordingly. This kind of reflective process is conducive to our fulfillment and requires that we experience the world as it is.

Now are these things important to us because we want them, as a desire satisfaction theorist would suggest; or do we want them for some reason regarding their nature? That is, do our lives go better because in having such things we feel satisfied? Or do our lives go better because those things are worth having? Nozick takes the latter position. In a comment on his own thought-experiment written several years after its first appearance, Nozick writes:

> Notice that I am not saying simply that since we desire connection to actuality the experience machine is defective because it does not give us what we desire . . . for that would make "getting whatever you desire" the primary standard. Rather, I am saying that the connection to actuality is important whether or not we desire it—that is why we desire it—and the experience machine is inadequate because it doesn't give us that.[6]

The argument here is that the connection to the actual world is an objective good in itself and so for that reason is desirable and ought to be desired. The experience machine disallows the connection and that is why hooking up to it thwarts the possibility of human fulfillment.

Under this view, the condition for the possibility of achieving the good life is that we confront the world as it actually is. We could have pleasurable experiences and satisfied desires that bear no attachment to the circumstances that obtain in the world. If we took those to be what has ultimate value for us, we would seemingly have to deny that actually doing things, being certain kinds of persons, and living in a natural world with others have any bearing on our well-being and happiness. Human fulfillment would be nothing more than the sum total of pleasurable experiences or satisfied desires. If, however, we believe that our fulfillment depends on our complex connection to the actual world and our attachments to others, then we are more likely to view happiness as a characteristically human achievement.

ENDNOTES

1. Peter Singer, ed. *Ethics* (Oxford University Press, 1994). See Singer's introduction to the section on Ultimate Good, p. 179.

2. Jeremy Bentham, *The Rationale of Reward* (originally published in 1825) in Singer, *Ethics,* p. 200.

3. John Stuart Mill, *Utilitarianism* (originally published in 1861); see Chapter 2 "What Utilitarianism Is." Reference here is from *The Philosophy of John Stuart Mill* edited by Marshall Cohen (Modern Library, 1961), pp. 331–332.

4. Stuart Rachels, *The Elements of Moral Philosophy* Eighth Edition (McGraw Hill, 2015), pp. 112–113.

5. Robert Nozick, *Anarchy, State, and Utopia* (Basic Books, 1974), pp. 43–45.

6. Robert Nozick, *The Examined Life: Philosophical Meditations* (Touchstone Books, 1990), pp. 106–107.

STUDY QUESTIONS

1. Distinguish between *instrumental* and *intrinsic goods.*
2. What role does consciousness play with respect to the concept of the good?
3. What is *hedonism*?
4. Explain Jeremy Bentham's *quantitative hedonism.* What is the *hedonistic calculus*?
5. Describe John Stuart Mill's *qualitative hedonism.* In what significant ways does Mill's theory differ from Bentham's? How does Mill distinguish between *higher* and *lower* pleasures?
6. Hedonism is a *monistic* view of the good. What does that mean? What is *value pluralism*?
7. What is *desire satisfaction theory*? How does it differ from hedonism?
8. How do Rachels and Nozick argue against hedonistic and desire-satisfaction theories?

QUESTIONS FOR REFLECTION

1. Do you think there is an ultimate good for us? If so, what is it?
2. Consider the question, *"Is it better to be a satisfied pig or a dissatisfied Socrates?"* How would Bentham and Mill answer the question? Who do you think has the better answer and why?
3. Is the good just a matter of feeling pleasure? Is it a matter of satisfying desires? Something else? Could your life be going badly even if you feel good or are satisfied? Is feeling good always what we want? (Think of Rachels's examples.)
4. Review Nozick's thought experiment about the *experience machine.* Would you connect to the machine? Why or why not?

SUGGESTIONS FOR FURTHER READING

Bramble, Ben. "The Experience Machine." *Philosophy Compass* 11 (3), 2016.

Crisp, Roger. "Pleasure Is All That Matters." *Think* 3 (7), 2004.

Feldman, Fred. *What is This Thing Called Happiness?*. Oxford: Oxford University Press, 2010.

Feldman, Fred. *Pleasure and the Good Life: Concerning the Nature, Varieties and Plausibility of Hedonism*. Oxford: Clarendon Press, 2004.

Fletcher, Guy, ed. *The Routledge Handbook of Philosophy of Well-Being*. Routledge, 2016.

Moore, G. E. *Principia Ethica*. Cambridge: Cambridge University Press, 1903.

Parfit, Derek. *Reasons and Persons*. Oxford: Oxford University Press, 1984.

Ross, W. D. *The Right and the Good*. Oxford: Clarendon Press, 1930.

chapter 4

Utilitarianism

Utilitarianism, as discussed in the previous chapter, is rooted in a theory of value. It seeks to identify in the first instance, what counts as good for us. Jeremy Bentham and John Stuart Mill, despite the respective differences in their views regarding the quantitative or qualitative approach to pleasure, are both hedonists in that they argue that pleasure and pleasure alone is desirable as an end in itself. It was also noted in the discussion that utilitarianism is the kind of normative ethical theory called *consequentialism*—a theory of right conduct that determines the rightness or wrongness of actions in terms of outcomes or consequences of actions. For the utilitarian, the concept of the good and the idea that consequences determine moral rightness and wrongness go hand-in-hand. The goal of moral action is to bring about the good, not just for oneself but for the greatest number. For the hedonistic utilitarians, then, pleasure has intrinsic value and is worth pursuing, and moral action should maximize pleasure (or at the very least minimize pain) for the greatest number of those affected by an action. As a consequentialist theory, utilitarianism says that an action is morally right when it succeeds in maximizing the good (or minimizing the bad if that's the best alternative) and wrong when it fails to do so. In short, utilitarianism says that what is morally right depends on a prior notion of what is intrinsically good. The focus of the previous chapter was on the concept of the good; the emphasis in this chapter is on utilitarianism as a theory of right conduct, and so the focus is on the concept of consequences as the criterion for morally correct action.

Utilitarianism has a rather elegantly simple conception of the purpose of morality. The point of moral action is to produce a circumstance where more people are made better off, where the good is distributed in such a way that a maximum number of people benefit from our actions. In this way, the utilitarian understands morality fundamentally as a way of improving the world. This is a way of understanding, in the most general terms possible, the point of consequentialism. What matters is the circumstance produced by actions, not the intentions behind our actions or even whether an action consists with a common sense view of morality that might involve concepts like rules, rights, and obligations. For the utilitarian, the only rule of morality is to perform actions that result in maximizing the overall good in the world.

Let's consider consequentialism a bit more precisely. Utilitarian theory holds that the evaluation of actions is determined exclusively in terms of the consequences they produce; the morality of an action is determined solely through an assessment of its consequences and nothing else. Our only obligation or duty in any situation is to perform that action, from among the alternative courses of action, which will result in the greatest possible balance of good over evil. Notice that this is an obligation or duty in the most abstract sense in that it really doesn't say which specific actions are right or wrong but only how it is that any action is right or wrong. The right thing to do, in any situation, is whatever would produce the best overall outcome for all those who will be affected by your action. The morally right action, the one we ought to perform, is the one that produces the best overall consequences for everyone.

What's important in utilitarian consequentialism is not necessarily who enjoys the benefits, but only that the net outcome is positive. Each person's benefit is equally important, so what matters is the overall good that is produced. Despite the apparent simplicity of the utilitarian approach, it actually requires a great deal of moral effort to achieve the goal of maximizing benefit. Utilitarianism requires that we always do the most we can to ensure that the good is distributed in such a way that the greatest number benefit. This makes morality a strenuous exercise, as we should never be content with only having done the minimum. Moreover, it requires that we set aside our own interests and the interests of those close to us and view ourselves and **all** others (not just those close to us) as equal in the capacity to be beneficiaries of moral action.

It is important also to see just what is excluded in the consequentialist's analysis of the morality of actions. To say that the overall good produced by an action is the exclusive determinant of an action's rightness or wrongness, is to deny any value to other concepts that typically play a role in our common sense notion of morality, concepts like intention, duty, the intrinsic worth of an action, or even one's character. From the consequentialist perspective, intentions are irrelevant in moral assessments. An action could very well have positive or negative unintended consequences and the action would be deemed right or wrong irrespective of what was intended in performing it. It also wouldn't make sense to say that an action is right or wrong in and of itself or that we have a duty to perform or refrain from performing certain actions independently of the outcomes of those actions, since that would be to exclude consequences from our moral assessments. In this respect, consequentialism is distinguished from duty ethics or *deontology*. It is also distinguished from *virtue ethics,* which emphasizes the moral qualities a person cultivates in himself or herself. A person's character doesn't matter to the consequentialist in that one does not have to be a virtuous person, or any sort of person in particular for that matter, to perform actions that wind up having good results. Whether it's likely that a person of bad character or with bad intentions will consistently perform actions with overall positive consequences is another matter. What is important here is that it is simply possible for such a person to do so. As we will see, such exclusions form the basis of some serious criticisms of utilitarianism.

In so far as it provides what it takes to be an objective and person-neutral criterion for the determination of moral rightness and wrongness, utilitarianism conceives of moral theory as kind of "science" of action. All we need do to meet the demands of the theory is to determine, from among all possible courses of action we could take, that action that will have the greatest overall positive outcome. Assuming people agree that the purpose of morality is, in fact, to produce optimific results and improve the circumstances in the world, utilitarianism employs a decision procedure that leads to ethical conclusions, free of subjective interests and which, when viewed in light of objective criteria, should settle our moral disagreements. Is it possible to arrive at the kind of certainty about outcomes that utilitarian theory seems to demand? And, even if it were possible to do so, would we have succeeded in explaining the moral life? Is morality simply about actions and consequences? What, if anything, might a moral theory have to say about intentions, obligations, and character?

Utilitarian Decision-Making

Recall Bentham's quantitative hedonism and his idea that it is possible to ascribe numerical values to pleasure and pain states according to certain criteria: *Intensity, duration, certainty, propinquity, fecundity, purity,* and *extent.* With respect to determining the utility of an action—its tendency to produce good consequences—and hence which course of action we should take, Bentham recommends the following procedure: Imagine that an action affects a certain number of persons (the extent) whose interests are concerned. For each individual affected by an action compute a value for each pleasure and pain in terms of each criterion—how deeply felt, how long lasting, how near or remote, how likely to produce sensations of the same sort or opposite sort, etc. Then sum up the value of each pleasure and sum up the value of each pain for each individual; if the sum of pleasure is greater, then the action has positive utility for an individual; if the sum of pain is greater than that of pleasure, then the action has negative utility for an individual. Once done for each individual, then sum up the numbers representing those who are positively affected and the numbers representing those negatively affected. This will give the utility of an action in terms of how it affects an entire community of individuals—the good tendency of the act is determined by a positive net balance of pleasure over pain; the bad tendency of an act is determined by a net balance of pain over pleasure. The moral demand: Perform that action which has the greatest net positive balance of pleasure (good) over pain (evil).[1]

Is it really conceivable that we should be required to employ this kind of analysis prior to making a moral judgment or ethical decision to act? By the time the process were complete and future results predicted, with no guarantee that they will occur, the need to act at all might have long passed. Bentham anticipates such concerns when he writes that:

> It is not to be expected that this process be strictly pursued previously to every moral judgment . . . It may, however, be always kept in view: and as near as the process actually pursued on these occasions approaches to it, so near will such process approach to the character of an exact one.[2]

How do or can we even know precisely how other individuals will be affected by our actions? Shouldn't morality be grounded on surer footing than the possibility or presumed likelihood of future outcomes? Is it even desirable at all to think of moral theory as an "exact science"? Wouldn't we be paralyzed by the process and perhaps cause greater harm in not acting as a result?

The issue is further complicated when we consider Mill's conception of qualitatively better forms of pleasure, as it is impossible to measure such pleasure in terms of magnitudes. But even if we reject the quantitative approach and the algorithmic decision procedure that attends it, we might still adopt the kind of heuristic contained in the quote from Bentham above. That is, while it is hardly likely that we could think of every possible consequence an action would have for an entire population of individuals, we should consider how they could conceivably be affected by our actions. We may have an intuitive sense about minimizing suffering and become more acutely aware of employing the utilitarian criterion of rightness with developed experience of acting in the world.

Take, for example, a simple version of the famous thought experiment called the *trolley problem*.[3] A trolley is barreling down a track out of control. On the track ahead in direct line of the runaway trolley are four workers who will be unable to get out of the way by the time the trolley reaches their position. All four will certainly be killed if the trolley hits them. There is, however, a switch that will divert the trolley onto a side track. You are standing at the switch and realize you can divert the trolley by flipping the switch. You also notice that there is a single individual on the side track who will certainly be killed if the trolley is diverted. Given this circumstance, should you pull the switch?

Many people, without much hesitation, say that the right thing to do is to pull the switch and divert the trolley even with the knowledge that one person will certainly be killed. Why so? In the first place, it seems to involve a simple calculation: The death of four people is worse than the death of one. But there's more to it. If you could prevent the worse outcome, then you ought to do so. Moreover, you ought to do so even though you are not directly responsible for what happens as a result of the trolley running out of control and even in knowing that the death of the person on the side track is the direct result of an action (flipping the switch) you took. There is not enough time to apply the utilitarian calculus in this case, even with such a small population to consider, but, as Bentham suggests, it is "kept in view." The situation, particularly the experience you have of being at the switch, triggers the moral intuition about minimizing suffering and the utilitarian criterion of rightness provides a justification for pulling the switch and diverting the trolley towards a single individual. Again what matters is the positive outcome, in this case fewer dead people.

But is the outcome really the only thing that matters? Does it matter, for instance, how it is that the people in the trolley example would come to be killed? If you pull the switch, then you have aimed the trolley at a single individual and thus would have killed that person. This is not necessarily to make a moral judgment, rather simply to state a fact. If you don't pull the switch, then you would have killed no one, but you would have let four people die. That said, there may be a moral difference between killing and letting die. If we go by the numbers alone, it seems that it is simply worse to let four die than to kill one. If, however, we believe that killing one may be worse than letting four people die, then something other than outcomes would matter in our moral decision making. One might hold to a moral principle like "killing is wrong" and believe that we ought not to perform wrong actions even to bring out good consequences. Perhaps changes in the circumstances may lead to shifting judgments even given the same net outcome.

Consider the same trolley scenario but suppose there was no switch and you could stop the trolley by pushing a person in front of it; or you could stop the trolley by jumping in front of it yourself—in either case, the other person or you will die and the four workers will not be killed. Should you push the person? Should you jump? Is there really any difference between pulling a switch and aiming a trolley at a person or pushing a person in front of a trolley if the outcome is the same? And if the outcome is all that matters shouldn't you jump in front of the trolley? Remember from the utilitarian perspective everyone's interests count equally. Or imagine the exact same scenario but with this difference: The single individual on the side track happens to be your aunt, whom you love dearly. Should it make any difference that the person on the side track is a family member? Should your emotional attachment to that person be a factor? Do you have special obligations to family members that must factor alongside any consideration of consequences?

In keeping the outcome the same while shifting the circumstances, we begin to see that there are problems with utilitarianism, even in a case where a simple calculation or intuition initially produced what appeared to be an obvious solution to the problem. This calls into question the universal applicability of the utilitarian criterion of moral rightness. There is at least a tension in the effort to apply utilitarian decision making across the board. In response to this, some utilitarians retrench and reaffirm the idea that consequences are all that matter; others attempt to temper the tension by introducing rules into the mix.

Act-Utilitarianism and Rule-Utilitarianism

It is standard practice to distinguish between two fundamental forms of utilitarianism, *act-utilitarianism* and *rule-utilitarianism*. Since these are both forms of utilitarianism, there is a common element in them. Both are consequentialist theories in that they hold the idea that moral rightness and wrongness are determined by outcomes and both accept the view that the purpose of morality is to improve the circumstances in the world, to bring about the greatest good for the greatest number. They differ significantly in terms of what counts when determining the consequences of actions. Begin with these basic definitions:

> *Act-utilitarianism* is the view that an action is right or wrong based **solely** on the consequences of that action itself.

> *Rule-utilitarianism* is the view that an action is right or wrong depending on whether it conforms to a general moral rule, obedience to which tends to bring about good consequences.

Act-utilitarianism is a pure form of utilitarianism. It denies that there is any way to determine the morality of actions independently of consequences. Each act is taken on its own and in its own situation. Except for the imperative to perform actions that, as far as we can reasonably predict, will produce optimal outcomes, there is no need to introduce general moral rules that range over classes of actions irrespective of the situation in which an action is performed. In effect, act utilitarianism says that the best chance we have to improve the general circumstances of the world is to consider each act individually. If we perform actions in each situation that bring about the best overall consequences and then add all those consequences together, it follows from the act-utilitarian perspective that we will have made the world a better place.

Rule-utilitarianism adopts the view that general moral rules must play a role in the determination of consequences. A particular action is viewed not solely in the context of its situation but in terms of whether it adheres to a general moral rule (e.g., always keep your promises). The moral rule itself, however, is not isolated from consequences; its value precisely as a rule is measured by the fact that, in general, obedience to the rule is the best way of assuring that good outcomes are produced. In this way, rule-utilitarianism is a theory that combines the core idea of consequentialism with a deontological element—the idea that we have certain moral obligations that obtain irrespective of any particular situation in which we may find ourselves.

Act-utilitarians argue that rule-utilitarianism is incoherent. Consider what happens in a situation where obedience to a rule conflicts with bringing about the best overall consequences. What should a rule-utilitarian do in that circumstance? Follow the rule or bring about good consequences? If rule-utilitarianism says that we should still follow the rule even though the best overall consequences in that situation would not result, then this would be to undermine the consequentialist aspect of the theory. It's hard to see how this counts as utilitarianism any longer. Does it help to respond, as a rule-utilitarian might, that it's not each specific application of a rule that matters but that, in general, obedience to the rule brings about the best consequences? So even in the case of conflict between the rule and consequences, it is best to obey the rule because the world is better if most people do so. The act-utilitarian argues that this still violates the fundamental principle of utilitarianism that in each case where we are to act we should strive to generate the best overall consequences. In settling the rule-consequences conflict this way, the rule-utilitarian values rules more than consequences. What if the conflict is settled on the side of consequences? A rule-utilitarian could argue that some particular situation is exactly the sort that requires us to make an exception to a rule. We might even amend the rule and say, "always obey the rule, except in situations like . . . ." In this case, the rule-utilitarian is opting for consequences over the rule. The act-utilitarian argues that it is practically impossible to foresee all such instances where exceptions would be allowed, and so it would not be possible to build all exceptions into a general rule. The rule would die the death of a thousand exceptions. If that's the case, then we should just go with act-utilitarianism and let the situation dictate.

In sum, act-utilitarianism argues that rule-utilitarianism is either a form of duty ethics, in which case it is inconsistent with consequentialism or it simply reduces to act-utilitarianism by opting for consequences over rules in specific situations. From this perspective, it seems that the only consistent and coherent form of utilitarianism is act-utilitarianism.[4]

But is this really the final word? Does act-utilitarianism fare any better as a moral theory than rule-utilitarianism? Let's consider two cases of the sort philosophers commonly construct that might shed further light on the matter:

> *The case of the deathbed promise:* Your grandfather, a very wealthy man, has named you in his will and you stand to inherit ten million dollars when he dies. He is a strong supporter of second amendment rights and a generous contributor to the National Rifle Association. With no time to change his will, on his deathbed, he asks you to promise that you will contribute one million dollars to the NRA upon receiving your inheritance. You make the promise; your grandfather dies. You are not especially in favor of the NRA, and when you receive your inheritance, you determine that the money could be put to better use by donating it to the Save the Children Fund, helping children in developing countries. What should you do, keep your promise or do more good by helping children?

The case of the unwitting homeless organ donor: A homeless man enters a hospital emergency room to have a cut on his leg stitched and treated. Upon examination, the attending doctor finds the man completely healthy. In the hospital are three people waiting for transplants, one needs a kidney, one a heart, and one a lung; they will die soon if they do not receive donor organs. It just so happens that the homeless man is a match for all three. The doctor decides that he should kill the homeless man, remove his organs, and save the three transplant patients. After all, he reasons, think of the good consequences, the three patients will survive and enjoy their lives, their families will be happy, and besides no one would even notice that the homeless man was gone. Did the doctor do the morally right thing?

Factoring consequences alone, the act-utilitarian has pat answers in both cases: Break your promise and kill one to save three. This presents a difficulty for act-utilitarianism in that the theory seemingly allows for actions which are wrong from a straightforward common conception of morality, which includes moral convictions like it is right to keep your promises (however uncomfortable it might be to do so) and wrong to kill the innocent (even if good consequences result from the act). In certain cases, then, act-utilitarianism would require us to perform actions that violate our firmly held moral beliefs. Should we just "bite the bullet," as the expression goes, and sacrifice our convictions for end results?

Now it looks as if rule-utilitarianism might provide the better responses in these two situations. It asks us to consider what the consequences would be if everyone decided not to keep promises when it was uncomfortable to do so or if doctors routinely killed unwitting homeless people to save the lives of others. Though this line of reasoning has the benefit of being more consistent with our ordinary moral conceptions, it still may not yet be sufficient in terms of justifying why we hold our moral rules to be valuable. Perhaps there are more fundamental reasons why we value moral rules. In the case of promise keeping, for instance, it could be that we simply owe it to others to do what the promise says we will do; or that keeping promises is a form of honesty and we value honesty; or, pertaining to the case above, that we view a deathbed promise as a solemn vow, or that we have unique obligations to our grandparents. We might believe that it is wrong to kill the innocent not because of the consequences that might be produced if it became a general practice, but because a person has a right to his or life.

The point here is that the reasons for valuing and following moral rules could be construed as independent of the outcomes of acting according to those rules. The issue is not only about choosing one form of utilitarianism over another, but rather whether any form of utilitarianism is adequate as a moral theory. We turn now to some criticisms of utilitarianism.

Some Criticisms of Utilitarianism

Throughout the preceding remarks, there are indications of serious flaws in utilitarian theory. As we have seen, utilitarianism, in so far as it is a form of consequentialism, makes right action parasitic on a prior concept of the good. In this way what is right is most generally understood as the means to bring about desired ends. The criticisms of utilitarianism are, in the main, directed against its core idea that consequences are the exclusive determinate of the morality of our actions. Are there no other morally relevant constraints on our actions? In terms of outcomes, utilitarianism regards each individual recipient of benefit as equal to any other. Is an optimal distribution of good all that matters, or should we consider who deserves what? Can utilitarianism account for justice without an adequate conception of desert? Utilitarianism might be too demanding in that we are often incapable of foreseeing all the consequences of our actions and would nonetheless be held accountable for their outcomes, and demanding in the sense that it requires us to "bite the bullet" with respect to deeply held moral convictions or even sacrifice those dear to us or perhaps even ourselves for the sake of a greater good. Shouldn't an adequate moral

theory allow us to act on our deepest convictions and treat ourselves and those close to us differently than we treat strangers?
Utilitarianism eschews any substantive notion of obligation or
duty. But mightn't we have general obligations and special obligations to certain individuals? Intentions and character have no
place in a utilitarian calculation. We might, however, believe that
these are greater determinants of the morality of our actions than
consequences. We may have unique capacities and commitments.
Should we give these up in favor of good outcomes? And finally
utilitarianism holds us accountable for the consequences not only
of our actions, but of our inaction and, in certain situations, even
for the consequences of the actions of others, without any real distinction among these. Aren't we uniquely responsible for our own
actions? Consideration of such questions points to some of the
main problems with utilitarian moral theory. What follows is a
brief summary of some central criticisms of that theory.

Utilitarianism is too demanding. There are several senses in which
utilitarian is too demanding. In the first instance, it seems to
require that we compute consequences for every action we take.
Since actions are neither right nor wrong in themselves, actions
are granted moral value only in terms of their results. But anything
we do has the potential to generate good or bad consequences;
therefore it would follow that any action, given a specific set of
circumstances, can be morally right or morally wrong. If this were
the case, we would be little more than consequence calculating
devices. Following from this, we could never really be certain that
the results we expect are those that will actually occur, and though
it might be the case that acting on expected results is morally
praiseworthy, it still may be possible that bad consequences result,
in which case we would have acted badly and be held accountable
for generating bad consequences. Here's a classic example of this:
You save a drowning man with expected good consequences. The
man you saved turns out to be Adolf Hitler. Wouldn't it have been
better for the world to have let Hitler drown. There seems to be
no assurance that we can get expected results and actual results to
line up all the time. Moreover, utilitarianism is overly demanding
in that it requires us to treat everyone with complete impartial-

ity—no one, yourself, your family, your friends, counts any more or any less than anyone else. Each individual is counted simply as a neutral element in the consequentialist calculation. Think of the versions of the trolley problem where you can stop the trolley by jumping in front of it or stop it by directing it toward your aunt. In either case, it would seem utilitarianism requires you to do those things. Is it really possible to meet the requirement of complete impartiality under such circumstances?

Utilitarianism requires that we give up on certain fundamental moral concepts. The common conception of morality includes certain concepts that utilitarianism rejects—e.g., moral obligation, rights, and justice. Rejecting such concepts may lead to performing actions that are morally wrong, that violate fundamental rights, and that constitute or lead to serious injustices. Since no action is right or wrong in itself, it's possible that utilitarianism would require us to perform an action that the common conception of morality holds to be simply wrong—break a promise, kill an innocent person, steal another's property, etc. Under an ordinary view of morality, refraining from such actions is morally obligatory because they disrespect persons, infringe on a person's rights or otherwise violate some objective (or at least believed to be objective) moral principle. Think again of the doctor who kills the homeless man to harvest his organs for transplants. If the man has a right to life, then it is a clear violation of his rights to kill him. Rights impose constraints on our actions in the sense that possible courses of action, and hence some consequential outcomes, are morally unacceptable and thus ruled out. It is a serious injustice to use people as neutral devices in a consequentialist calculation, even if the results are optimal in that circumstance. Injustices may also follow from the utilitarian commitment to impartiality in outcomes. Is it simply the pattern of distribution that matters morally or does it make a difference who deserves to reap benefits and reward and who deserves ill? For the utilitarian it doesn't matter so long as the numbers work. No adequate moral theory should require morally wrong actions, violations of rights, and serious injustices. Utilitarianism might, at times, require these.

Utilitarianism adopts a notion of negative responsibility. This criticism comes from Bernard Williams's critique of utilitarianism.[5] Williams asks us to imagine the following scenario: Jim, a botanist, is on an expedition in a South American country. He stumbles upon a warlord, Pedro, who is about to kill twenty Indians. Pedro says to Jim if you shoot one Indian, I will let the other nineteen go. If Jim doesn't shoot the one, Pedro will shoot all twenty. What should Jim do? The ready-made utilitarian response is that, of course, Jim should shoot the one Indian, for in doing so he will have brought about better consequences than the alternative where Pedro shoots all twenty. What if Jim doesn't shoot the one Indian? Then, in some sense, utilitarianism holds him responsible. It's important to see just what this means. It's not merely that Jim would be responsible for the consequences of his inaction, as one might be if he did nothing to save a drowning baby. More than that Jim is responsible for the outcomes of an action that someone else performs. This seems to run completely counter to our ordinary notion of moral responsibility, which says we are accountable for our own actions and sometimes for omissions, but not that we are ever responsible for the outcomes of some other person's actions. Williams argues that consequentialism embraces a strong notion of negative responsibility; he defines negative responsibility in this way: "... if I know that if I do X, O_1 will eventuate, and if I refrain from doing X, O_2 will [eventuate], and that O_2 is worse than O_1, then I am responsible for O_2 if I refrain voluntarily from doing X."[6] It's one thing to say that Jim could have prevented the worse occurrence, but quite another to assert that he is responsible in the sense that his choice not to kill one Indian somehow made the worse occurrence happen. In the example, Pedro's actions—not Jim's inaction—directly produced the worse outcome. To hold Jim responsible in the same way is absurd. Utilitarianism cannot account for how it is that each of us is uniquely responsible for his or her actions and not responsible for the actions of others.

Utilitarianism violates personal integrity. This is also a major point in Williams's critique of utilitarianism.[7] Here is a simplified account of his concept of integrity. We have projects and deeply held commitments that define us as the kinds of persons we are and which motivate us to act. These projects and commitments have deep moral value for us and cannot be measured like pleasures in a utilitarian calculus nor understood from the perspective of utilitarian impartiality. Personal integrity is achieved in the pursuit of those projects and commitments. An adequate moral theory must take into account that one's projects and commitments have a normative dimension—think of the difference between Jim and Pedro, a botanist and a warlord—and that, most generally, one's actions need to be reflective of those projects and commitments. Utilitarianism requires Jim to act in a way inconsistent with his commitments, his most deeply held moral convictions. It requires him to give up on his personal moral commitments in favor of someone else's moral projects. Should we be required to do this whenever circumstances demand it? Utilitarianism suggests so. But this is the opposite of integrity. Integrity requires that people hold to their considered moral judgments and act in pursuit of their projects and commitments. Williams writes:

> It is absurd to demand of such a man [i.e., a person who possesses integrity], when the sums come in from the utility network which the projects of others have in part determined, that he should just step aside from his own project and decision and acknowledge the decision which utilitarian calculation requires. It is to alienate him in a real sense from his actions and the source of his action in his own convictions. It is to make him into a channel between the input of everyone's projects, including his own, and an output of optimific decisions; but this is to neglect the extent to which *his* actions and *his* decisions have to be seen as the actions and decisions which flow from the projects and attitudes with which he is most clearly identified. It is thus, in the most literal sense, an attack on his integrity.[8]

Utilitarianism, then, with its emphasis on impartiality and its doctrine of negative responsibility divorces a person from his or her own moral convictions and places that person anywhere he or she might fit to meet the demands of a consequentialist calculation. This would be to deny any central role to integrity in the moral life.

A final thought about utilitarianism: What initially appears to be an elegantly simple idea about the purpose of morality—to make circumstances better for as many as possible—turns out to be extraordinarily complex and deeply flawed as a moral theory.

ENDNOTES

1. Jeremy Bentham, *Introduction to the Principles of Morals and Legislation* (Hafner, 1948), pp. 29–31. This work was originally published in 1789.
2. Bentham, p. 31.
3. The trolley problem was introduced by Phillipa Foot in her essay "The Problem of Abortion and the Doctrine of Double Effect" in *Virtues and Vices and Other Essays in Moral Philosophy* (Basil Blackwell, 1978). Judith Jarvis Thomson gives an extended analysis of this thought experiment in "The Trolley Problem" published in *The Yale Law Journal*, Vol. 94, No. 6 (May, 1985), pp. 1395–1415.
4. J. J. C. Smart, "An Outline of A System of Utilitarian Ethics" in J. J. C. Smart and Bernard Williams, *Utilitarinaism: For and Against,* (Cambridge University Press, 1973), pp. 3–74. See especially section 2 on act-utilitarianism and rule-utilitarianism, pp. 9–12. There Smart argues that rule-utilitarianism, in opting for rules over consequences, is a form of what he calls "rule worship".
5. Bernard Williams, "A Critique of Utilitarianism" in Smart and Williams, *Utilitarianism: For and Against,* pp. 77–150. See especially section 3 on negative responsibility, pp. 93–100.

6. Bernard Williams, p. 108.
7. See especially Williams on the concept of integrity, section 5 of his critique of utilitarianism, pp. 108–118.
8. Bernard Williams, pp. 116–117.

STUDY QUESTIONS

1. Distinguish between *consequentialism* and *deontology*.
2. In what sense is utilitarianism a consequentialist moral theory? Explain in detail how a utilitarian would decide whether or not an act is morally right?
3. What, according to utilitarianism, is the purpose of morality?
4. Explain the difference between *act-utilitarianism* and *rule-utilitarianism*.
5. Summarize the main arguments against utilitarianism.
6. What is the idea of *negative responsibility*? Consider the case of Jim and the Indians.
7. Describe Bernard Williams's idea of integrity.

QUESTIONS FOR REFLECTION

1. What is the *trolley problem*? Consider utilitarian responses to each of the following scenarios:
   a) pulling the switch and directing the trolley onto a side track, killing a person
   b) pushing a large person in front of the trolley
   c) jumping in front of the trolley yourself
   d) pulling the switch and directing the trolley onto a side track toward your aunt

   What would you do in each case? Give reasons for you answers.

2. Do you think we are ever responsible for the consequences of someone else's actions?

3. Utilitarianism embraces a strong notion of impartiality—everyone's interests count equally. If utilitarianism is true, then shouldn't we all sacrifice something to help anyone (those who are starving, for instance) in need? Or are we entitled to give greater weight to our own interests and those close to us? What do you think?

SUGGESTIONS FOR FURTHER READING

Bentham, Jeremy. *Introduction to the Principles of Morals and Legislation* [1789]. New York: Hafner, 1948.

Darwall, Stephen. *Consequentialism*. Oxford: Blackwell Publishing, 2003.

Eggleston, Ben & Miller, Dale E. eds. *The Cambridge Companion to Utilitarianism*. Cambridge: Cambridge University Press, 2014.

Foot, Philippa. "The Problem of Abortion and the Doctrine of Double Effect." *Oxford Review* 5, 1967.

Mill, John Stuart (Roger Crisp, ed.), *Utilitarianism* [1861]. Oxford: Oxford University Press, 1998.

Moore, G. E. *Principia Ethica* [1903]. Cambridge: Cambridge University Press, 1993.

Sidgwick, Henry. 1907. *The Methods of Ethics*, Seventh Edition [1907]. Indianapolis: Hackett Publishing Company, 1981.

Singer, Peter. "Famine, Affluence, and Morality." *Philosophy and Public Affairs.* 1(3), 1972.

Thomson, Judith Jarvis. "*The Trolley Problem.*" 94 Yale Law Journal, 1985.

Williams, Bernard. "Persons, Character, and Morality," in Bernard Williams, *Moral Luck*. Cambridge: Cambridge University Press, 1981.

chapter 5

Duty

When you think about morality, do you think more about desires, inclinations, making people feel good, and bringing about good consequences, or do you think more about duty, rules, intentions, and the quality of certain actions themselves? Do you think that actions serve as means to some end or do you think of actions as being simply right or wrong? If someone poses a question like, "Is it wrong to lie?" are you more likely to answer, "That depends," or "Absolutely, it's always wrong to lie"? Do you think our moral reason is limited by our natural desires and our ability to predict consequences of our actions or do you believe that moral reason is independent of human desire and can lead us to understand why certain actions are right or wrong in themselves? Do you think actions are only right or wrong in terms of what they achieve or fail to achieve, or do you think that what one intends to do matters in our moral assessment of actions? Do you think we could be "negatively responsible" for the consequences of someone else's action or do you think we are uniquely responsible for our own actions?

The collection of these questions is designed to show the stark contrast between consequentialist theories like utilitarianism and deontological moral theories or duty ethics. Deontology (from the Greek *deon*, meaning obligation or duty) is the philosophical term used to refer to the kind of moral theory in which the concept of duty is fundamental. Under this view, the rightness or wrongness of actions is not dependent on outcomes, but rather is intrinsic to an action itself. We have duties to perform right actions and duties to refrain from performing wrong actions. Since deontology rejects the idea that consequences justify the claim that an action is morally right or morally wrong, it requires a different form of justification, one that provides us with a way of knowing just what kinds of actions are duties. In this regard, the concept of moral rightness takes priority over the concept of good. It is the task of deontology to explain why this is so and how it is that we have moral obligations or duties at all. For the deontologist, moral obligations are objective in the sense that they apply to all persons, and so it is important also to account for the general applicability of moral principles.

Consider too that there is a deontological aspect to our everyday moral experience. Many people believe that it is necessary to meet the demands of their moral principles and do the right thing, even if it doesn't generate pleasure or happiness for themselves or others. Our desires to experience good things sometimes run counter to what we know is right to do on some occasion. This is not to suggest that the desire for pleasure or happiness is bad, or that those things are bad in themselves, but rather that what is morally right is independent of those things and our desire for them. It is also not to suggest that desire and duty are necessarily at odds or that doing what is right somehow requires feelings of displeasure. In an ideal moral universe, desires and duties would always coincide. The point again is that we don't derive our duties from our desires, and outcomes do not provide a reason for claiming that an action is right.

This is another way of viewing the contrast between deontology and consequentialism. Think of Bentham and Mill and their idea that morality is rooted in the fact that we desire pleasure and pleasure alone is what is desirable. Under their view, moral reason is limited to figuring out the best way to achieve the goal of bringing about the greatest good for the greatest number. Deontology holds an opposing view; the problem of morality is to determine what is right, and if we could accomplish that, then an even more challenging problem emerges: Assuming we know the right thing to do, why should we do it? The answer might simply be "because it's right." Moreover, we can know this in advance with some measure of certainty; there is no need to wait until the results are in, so to speak, before we have a clear sense of moral rightness.

If it's not the desire to bring about good consequences that constitutes moral motivation, then what should the moral motive be to do the right thing? Here deontologists often appeal to the concept of intention. In performing a morally right action one might intend certain consequences, but if consequences are not the determinant of rightness, then in having that intention one is not necessarily performing an action because it is the right thing. What if the consequences were different? What if a morally wrong action was more likely to bring about the desired ends? Here's an example to illustrate the point: Suppose Cynthia gives to charity, and does so in order to benefit from a tax deduction. Her motive here is self-interested and her intention in performing the act is to reap some benefit. She is not motivated to act because of the goodness of charitable giving, but because of what she stands to gain. Now suppose the tax deduction is taken away. So goes Cynthia's motive, but the goodness of charitable giving still remains. Cynthia realizes she can reap the same financial benefit by cheating on her taxes. Since she is motivated by self-interest and intends to perform the action because it benefits her, then she is likely to cheat on her taxes. But just as the lack of benefit doesn't change the intrinsic goodness of the act of charitable giving, so neither does the benefit Cynthia receives from cheating on her taxes change the intrinsic wrongness of that act. An action is right even without good consequences and an action is wrong even with good consequences.

We should then be motivated to act because an action is a duty; moral rightness itself should be the object of our intention. Actions are right or wrong in terms of whether they adhere to a clear moral rule; but for an action to have moral value it must be performed by a person whose intention is to do that action because it is the right thing to do. We certainly hold people responsible when they intend to perform morally wrong actions. That's just a clear case of immorality in both the action and in the bad intentions of the person. Deontology, as presented thus far, goes further in suggesting that right actions done for the wrong reasons (with improper motives and misdirected intentions) effectively lose their moral value. Adherence to a moral rule is a necessary but not a sufficient condition for one's actions to have moral value. It's important to see, then, that actions aren't made right by intentions. We couldn't just use intentions, for instance, to absolve a person of responsibility for performing evil deeds precisely because a person's full moral responsibility requires the recognition that an action is a duty. This, as we will see, is an essential aspect of the Kantian version of duty ethics.

In his highly influential work, *The Foundations of the Metaphysics of Morals* written in 1785, Immanuel Kant (1724–1804) argues that the foundation of morality is rationality itself. There he systematically attempts to demonstrate that moral duty cannot be derived from our natural tendencies, psychological inclinations, or subjective desires; nor could it be gotten on the basis of some idea of what outcomes our actions might produce. Instead duty must be grounded in reason itself. For Kant, morality requires that we act freely, that we choose to perform actions that we recognize to be morally good. We would be incapable of rationally choosing to act if there were conditions that imposed constraints on us from the outside. For Kant, morality requires that we be autonomous, self-directed agents.

In this chapter we will focus on Kant's approach as a paradigmatic example of deontological moral theory. Before considering Kant's view specifically, it is worth mentioning that there are other kinds of deontological theories, each of which attempts to explain how moral duties are to be understood. Here are several versions:

1. *The Divine Command Theory*: The divine command theory says that an action is morally right or wrong because it is commanded by God and because God

commands it we are under a moral obligation to do or refrain from doing what the command requires. So we ought to perform actions simply because they are duties as determined by God; whether or not they are consistent with our desires or bring about good consequences.

2. *Natural Law Ethics*: Natural law theory argues that there are certain things that are good for us by nature, and reason, the defining characteristic of human nature, tells us what they are. Moral or practical reasoning leads us to an understanding of what actions are required to achieve and sustain those goods; we have a duty to perform such actions. This is not to be confused with utilitarianism, where the concern is to bring about the best overall consequences for the greatest number. In contrast, the natural law theorist believes that fundamental goods are inherent in nature and so the actions that sustain those goods are absolutely required. Thomas Aquinas (1225–1274), for instance, argues that on the basis of this use of reason we can derive a general and fundamental principle of morality: "Do good and avoid evil." In applying this general principle to specific goods we can come up with moral rules that apply universally—this is the deontological element in natural law ethical theory. For example, life is a natural good. Morality would require us, then, to perform actions that are life-sustaining and avoid those that prevent the realization of or destroy that good. So on the basis of the general principle cited above, we could deduce that an action like murder is wrong, and not just sometimes, but universally. Note that natural law ethics is a mixed view. It does define the right in terms of a prior understanding of the good, but unlike consequentialism, it believes we can determine moral obligations in advance.

3. *Natural Rights Theory*: Natural rights theory suggests that, by nature, human beings are endowed with certain rights that are inalienable and that form the basis of our moral relationships to each other. John Locke (1632–1704),

for instance, identified such rights as life, liberty, and property. The deontological component here is that the rights of individuals impose obligations on others. If one has a right to life, then this minimally requires that we refrain from any actions which violate that right; one has a right not to be killed and this imposes an obligation on us not to kill; if one has a right to property, then we have an obligation not to steal, and so on. Moral duty is thus determined by the constraints that rights impose on our actions.

Kant rejects all of these kinds of theory, not because he disbelieves in God, or that he thinks there are no natural goods, or that he believes we have no rights. His point is that the ground for moral obligation is to be found in rationality alone, free from the constraints that nature imposes on us as human beings and independent even of God's commands, which in order to bind us morally would be rational themselves. Let's turn now to a discussion of the central ideas in Kant's moral theory.

Kantian Moral Theory

Kant's project is guided by the fundamental idea that if morality matters at all, it can only be because we are rational and free. Though there is much in human life that is subject to our desires, morality must, in some sense, be independent of those desires. The idea of freedom that serves as the basis for morality is not one that can be understood in terms of what we "want" to do, but rather needs to be understood in terms of what we "ought" to do. That is, Kant advocates the idea that freedom involves choosing to do what one rationally knows to be one's duty.

On the face of it, this is difficult to grasp because duty imposes a kind of necessity on us—an obligation to do or refrain from doing certain things. It would seem that this necessity conflicts with freedom in that obligation restricts our actions. Kant has it the other way around. True moral freedom is unrestricted by anything in nature, by our desires, by expected outcomes of actions, etc. Freedom is manifest in our rational capacity to choose moral-ity (duty) for ourselves. Our rational nature is in essence our autonomy—the idea that we can impose the moral law on our-selves. Note further that this means we can choose not to obey the dictates of moral reason, but we can't so choose and at the same time expect that our actions would have any moral value. This imposes on each of us a singularly unique moral responsibility to choose the right thing for the right reason. Moreover, this sense of moral freedom serves as a foundation for the universality of moral principles and duties. Rationality, though manifest in one's own choices, belongs to no one in particular. The rules it uncovers are rules that apply to everyone, irrespective of specific circumstances and situations. For Kant all of this adds up to the fundamental reason why we ought to choose to obey moral duty; namely, that in doing so we respect persons—ourselves and others—as ratio-nal, autonomous agents. In fine, Kant argues that morality is only possible for beings that are rational in this sense.

What follows is a brief summary of how Kant attempts to estab-lish this idea of morality, with a focus on three important Kantian concepts: The good will, the categorical imperative, and respect for persons.

The Good Will

Kant begins with the idea that a good will is the only thing that can be thought of as good without qualification or good in itself.[1] This does not mean that there are no other things that are good for us; there are plenty of such things. Kant, himself, identifies such goods as *talents of the mind* like intelligence, wit, and prudence, or *qualities of temperament* like courage, resoluteness, and perse-verance, and *blessings of fortune* like power, wealth, honor, health, and happiness. These are undoubtedly good things or traits to have, but the mere possession of them does not make the posses-sor good. This is to say that none of these things nor all of them combined measure up to something that is good without qualifi-cation. You can think, for instance, of an intelligent, witty, resolute, healthy **bank robber.** Or you can imagine an intelligent, prudent, perseverant, resolute, powerful, wealthy, healthy **tyrant.** It is evident that one can have these goods and use them for incredible evil. They are only good if qualified by a good will, a will that is directed solely toward moral goodness.

Certain emotional states seem especially well-designed for a good will—e.g., self-control and calm deliberation—and we generally admire such traits. Even these, however, are not unconditionally good and are admirable only if they are informed by a good will. If not informed by a good will, they "may become extremely bad." For instance, Kant says that "the coolness of a villain makes him not only far more dangerous but also more directly abominable in our eyes than he would have seemed without it."[2]

How, then, should we understand the idea that the good will is good without qualification? Here's Kant's sense of it. The good will is that will which chooses to act for the sole reason that it recognizes an action as the right thing to do. Much of Kant's moral philosophy is an expansion of the ideas contained in that statement. The good will *chooses.* In this sense, the good will is not defined by an emotional feeling, but by the exercise of freedom. So the good will is a free will. But it's not that the good will chooses whatever it wants. Our psychology tendencies, nature inclinations, and desires are better suited to get us what we want. To say that the good will is free is to say that it chooses to perform right actions. The good will is also a rational will. On the basis of reason, the good will *recognizes* that an action is the right thing to do. Finally, the good will is a will that has a proper motive or intention. It chooses to act *because* (for the reason that) an action is the right thing to do. Why do the right thing? Because it's the right thing. The good will, Kant says, has duty as its motive. The good will is a free, rational, and properly motivated will.

From this perspective, the good will is good in itself because it is impossible for it to choose anything other than what is morally right. It lays down the necessary and sufficient conditions for our actions to have moral value. This is to say that if a person has a good will, that person's actions would have moral worth in virtue of that will alone; and without a good will, a person's actions could not have moral worth. So the moral worth of actions is not determined by consequences.

In Kant's view, consequences neither add to nor subtract from the inherent value of the good will, since the good will is defined completely independent of any good or bad results that may be produced by our actions. Good consequences, for oneself or for the general welfare, could be produced by means other than moral action. A good will would thus be unnecessary if morality were founded on the satisfaction of desires or for the improvement of conditions in the world. Not even happiness counts as the ultimate goal of action; it is not the point of morality. Instead Kant suggests if one performs right actions for the right reason, then one is worthy of happiness even if one is not actually happy. By the same token, it is impossible to know the moral law without the rationality of a good will, since the very purpose of moral reason is to come to know what our moral obligations are. Morality is the exclusive province of rational beings. Any rational being—a human person or any other kind of being with the capacity to develop an autonomous good will—is bound by and judged by the same moral rules.

In choosing to perform an action because it is a duty, the good will makes duty its motive. In this sense, it is not sufficient simply to perform an action that happens to be in accordance with duty. Rather, to make duty the motive is, as Kant puts it, "to act from duty." So an action may be in accordance with duty, but still not be done with duty as the motive.

Here's an example to illustrate the distinction: Tom, Dick, and Harry are students in a moral philosophy class and they have written papers on Kant's moral theory. Tom and Harry submitted original work and both received reasonably good grades. Dick plagiarized his paper, was caught and received a failing grade for the course. Tom and Harry discuss Dick's action and agree that he got what he deserved, as he clearly did something wrong. Tom says that he wouldn't plagiarize because he fears getting caught and wouldn't want to suffer the same fate as Dick. Harry wonders whether Tom has learned anything from studying Kant and proclaims that's no reason not to plagiarize. He says the only reason not to plagiarize is to recognize that plagiarism is a form of dishonesty and one has a moral obligation to be honest. In other words, Harry says he didn't plagiarize because it's wrong to do so. It should be evident that Dick was just plain dishonest, and it seems clear enough that Harry and Tom both did the right thing. But did both of them act honestly?

Here's a trim Kantian analysis: Tom acted on the basis of an inclination not to get caught and a desire to avoid punishment. But what if he were sure he wouldn't get caught and could thus be certain that he would be spared the discomfort of any punishment? It might be, with those conditions no longer operative, that Tom would have plagiarized. Harry acted without regard to the consequences; his action was motivated by the rational judgment that plagiarism is downright dishonest. Harry's action meets the criteria of Kant's good will, but Tom's action does not. The Kantian conclusion is that Harry's action has moral worth, but Tom's does not. Notice further the full and rather stringent judgment that this involves. Harry is an honest person, but Tom is not. Tom, though his action was right, gets no more moral credit than Dick, whose action was clearly wrong.

Many might feel troubled by all this, particularly the last conclusion. After all, isn't it the case that doing the right thing, even if for the wrong reason, is preferable to doing the wrong thing? Kant's answer is a clear and resounding NO. The only way one would be inclined to say so is if consequences mattered in the determination of moral rightness, and recall if that were the case then rationality would not be required for moral action. In fine, Harry acted freely and rationally, but Tom did not.

It should be evident, then, that the reason one has for acting is crucial in the determination of moral value. The specific reason or rule or simple argument one gives for acting is what Kant calls a *maxim*. Kant is not saying that if we act on inclination, then the action we perform cannot be right. What he is saying is that inclination could never suffice as a moral reason for acting. The reason is that if you try to frame your maxim in terms of your inclinations, then you would have a rule that applies only to you. Since morality lays down universal obligations, then the maxim of your action ought to be one that any person could adopt. It is possible, for instance, to universalize the idea that one should always act honestly. Could the same be said for something like the following: Act honestly only when not doing so brings about bad consequences for you? If that were the rule, then one would have no reason to act honestly, if there were no bad consequences in acting dishonestly. But how would we know when our maxims determined our moral duties? In order to answer this, we turn to a discussion of Kant's supreme moral principle—the categorical imperative.

The Categorical Imperative[3]

Rules for acting are framed as imperatives or commands that tell us what to do and they are common in our everyday experience. "Take the 7:45 train!" "Brush your teeth!" "Shut the window!" "Study calculus!" "Zip up your fly!" There is an important aspect to these imperatives; namely, they are conditioned on some goal or other one wishes to achieve. For instance:

> "Take the 7:45 train to ensure that you get to Grand Central Station by 9:00."
>
> "Brush your teeth so you don't get cavities."
>
> "Shut the window so it doesn't get too cold in the room."
>
> "Study calculus so you can get your engineering degree."
>
> "Zip up your fly so your date doesn't think you're a slob or a pervert."

These imperatives apply to particular persons in specific situations. They pertain only in those circumstances where a particular person has a desire or inclination to reach some specified goal. They really go shorthand for conditional statements like: "If you want an engineering degree, then study calculus," or "If you want to be at Grand Central Station by 9:00, then take the 7:45 train," and so on. Kant calls these *hypothetical imperatives*. A hypothetical imperative is conditional in the sense that it depends on certain things, and tells us what needs to be done in order to attain some desired objective. A hypothetical imperative, like any command, is a rule of reason, but it dictates an action which is good only as a means to something else; it does not command us to perform an action which is good in itself. Indeed, it would certainly be odd to say something like "it is always right to take the 7:45 train." What if you don't need to be at Grand Central Station until 2:00 or what if you don't need or wish to be there at all?

Kant argues that hypothetical imperatives cannot function as moral imperatives. This is not to deny their value, as it is clear that we live by these sorts of imperatives on a daily basis. Rather, in setting up conditions, hypothetical imperatives do not command absolutely. For Kant, moral actions are not means to ends, but are just right or wrong in themselves. So he says that moral imperatives must command absolutely, with no conditions attached. He calls this kind of command the *categorical imperative*. In Kant's duty-based moral theory, the categorical imperative is what he considers to be the "supreme principle of morality." The categorical imperative is *unconditional* in that it commands absolutely without any reference to any consequence of an action. It applies to moral actions and determines the necessity of performing an action; that is, it determines an action to be a moral duty. It derives from rationality itself and is an expression of our autonomy as moral agents. Reason tells us what the moral law is and we impose that law on ourselves; this is the function of the good will in Kant's sense.

As Kant understands it, the categorical imperative is a general command and is used as a kind of test procedure for determining what specific actions qualify as moral duties. It says whatever action you take, if it is to qualify as a moral action, must exemplify certain inherent qualities. Specifically it must be the kind of action that does not depend on your particular interests or desires or goals, that is consistently performable in any circumstance whatsoever, that any rational person would perform, and that respects persons as rational, autonomous agents. This is best understood in terms of how the categorical imperative is formulated. Kant gives several formulations, two of which are as follows:

1. The Principle of Universalizability: *Act as if the maxim of your action were to become through your will a universal law of nature.*

2. The Principle of Respect for Persons: *Act in such a way that you always treat humanity, whether in your own person or in the person of any other, never simply as a means, but always at the same time as an end.*

Though these are different versions of the categorical imperative, they are not different commands just different expressions of the same command. They fundamentally say the same thing—always do what is right. In these formulations what is right is understood to be that which we can consistently will to be universal and that which respects persons as having value in themselves.

To see how the categorical imperative is used as a test procedure for determining what specific actions qualify as moral duties consider the principle of universalizability. To test for universalizability we can ask: "What would happen if everyone did this?" or, "Would it be okay for anyone to do this in the same or similar circumstances?" If what I am about to do is morally correct then, for Kant, it would be morally correct for everyone to do the same thing. This is precisely what it means for an action to be universalizable; that is, it is good for anyone and everyone, everywhere, at any time. More specifically, the categorical imperative says you should be *willing* to say that a moral rule applies to everyone, yourself included. You cannot be exempt from the demands of morality or expected to be treated differently than any other person. So for instance, if you are not willing to allow others to lie to you, then you ought not lie to others. Moreover, the rule must be applied consistently, if a rule leads to a contradiction, then it cannot be a valid moral rule. Suppose I wish to lie. If I will that lying become a universal law, then I must be prepared to say that it is logically possible that everyone can be lying all the time. But does that make logical sense? If I say that all persons are liars, then either I'm lying or telling the truth. If I'm telling the truth, then it can't be true that all persons are liars. If I'm lying, then it wouldn't be true that all persons are liars. Under such a circumstance no one could ever know who's lying and who's not; it would no longer be possible to trust anything anyone ever says. Kant famously concludes, "I can will to lie, but I cannot will that lying become a universal law." There is no inconsistency in willing that everyone be honest; truth-telling, for instance, can be universalized.

Kant distinguishes between two classes of duties. He calls these *perfect duties* and *imperfect duties*. *Perfect duties* are such that they can be universally willed and in breaking them we could clearly see a logical contradiction and would quite positively be disrespecting persons—ourselves or others. These are sometimes called *negative* duties in that they can be expressed as prohibitions such as don't murder; don't lie; don't steal; don't commit suicide. A rational will understands that we must never do such things because we could not will such acts as murder or lying or stealing or suicide to be universal, and in doing such things we would be treating persons as means to our own ends. *Imperfect duties* are not as specific as perfect duties in that they are broad imperatives that require us to use our wills in determining just how to obey them. These are sometimes called *positive* duties because to obey them requires more than just refraining from performing certain acts, it requires doing certain things.

When we disobey perfect duties, we clearly do something disrespectful to persons. In disobeying imperfect duties, we may not be actively disrespecting ourselves or others as in the case of breaking perfect duties, but neither would we be respecting those persons. Consider that we have an imperfect duty to help others in need or a duty to develop our talents. There are many ways to do these things and so we must decide for ourselves how best to meet those demands. It's easy to figure how not to murder someone, quite another matter to decide how to help someone. There is certainly a difference between setting a homeless man on fire and indifferently passing by him sitting on a park bench every day. If someone sets a homeless person on fire, that is a clear violation of a perfect duty. It's not simply that he has done nothing to help the homeless man, he has done something atrociously harmful. If you indifferently pass by, you are not actively doing anything to harm him, but neither are you doing anything actively to help him; this may constitute a violation of an imperfect duty. Also, we could imagine that no one ever obeyed imperfect duties; that is, disobedience to them does not issue in a straightforward logical contradiction. It's quite possible, for instance, that everyone could be lazy in a way that it is not possible for everyone to be a liar. But would you think of a world in which no one ever developed his or her talents to be a sufficiently robust moral community? With respect to perfect duties, we **couldn't** consistently will that breaking those duties be universalized; with respect to imperfect duties a rational person **wouldn't** will that breaking them be universalized. A rational person wouldn't will a world in which no one developed his talents and no one helped anyone in need, despite the fact that such a world may be logically possible. For Kant, both types of duties are required for the moral life. Morality requires not simply refraining from doing bad things, but actively doing good things as well, and the application of the categorical imperative determines what those duties are.

Respect for Persons

The second formulation of the categorical imperative, the principle of respect for persons, provides perhaps the best way of understanding the fullest expression of Kant's moral theory. In his view, persons have value and dignity in themselves and are thus worthy of respect.[4] This value is intrinsic and does not derive from any empirical circumstances, whether external situations or internal inclinations. What matters from the moral point of view is that persons are rational and free, and as such deserve to be treated as equal members of a moral community. A person's value comes not from being a member of a species, but from having the capacity to rationally determine duties and to be self-legislating autonomous agents. Any being that had such capacities would qualify, in Kant's sense, as a person and would count as a member of a universal moral community, what he refers to as a "kingdom of ends."

It might seem that Kant is denying a simple fact of our existence in saying that we should not treat persons as a means to an end. After all, don't we use the waitress in a restaurant as a means to get our food, or the mechanic as a means to repair our cars, or the musician as a means to please our ears, and so forth? On more careful examination, however, we find that Kant acknowledges this fact. His point is that we should never **simply** or **merely** use persons as means. It is possible to use people in the ways described above and still respect them and allow them to use us. The waitress brings our food, but she gets paid and we give her a tip. We use the mechanic to repair our car, but he uses us as the source of his livelihood. We use the musician for our pleasure, but he takes pleasure in playing to a large audience. We do these things out of mutual cooperation or perhaps even with a kind of mutual respect. What the Kantian view prohibits is using persons as if they were mere things.

When we use persons as things we deny their intrinsic value as rational, autonomous beings. We turn them into tools or devices used for the purpose of benefitting ourselves, where the other is incapacitated from benefitting from any mutual cooperation or participating in a community of mutual respect. Kidnapping a person and holding her for ransom, depriving someone of his liberty and using him as a slave, committing date rape, or stealing another person's property are all clear instances of using other persons as things. No rational person would consent to being a slave, a kidnap or rape victim, or to having his or her property stolen. But think also of more ordinary experiences. Jack and Jill have been dating for a while. Jill loves Jack, but Jack is just not sure about his feelings for Jill. They both need a place to live. Jill says she'd be happy to move in with Jack if he swears that he loves her. Jack's desperate for an affordable apartment and moving into a place with Jill would be ideal. He swears undying love, and Jill believes him. They get the apartment together. By trading on her trust and using it to his own advantage, Jack really views Jill as part of a real estate deal. (Coda: It is later revealed that Jack is a habitual liar and a cheat and Jill learns this and uncovers his self-regarding motive about the apartment; she's devastated.) We might say, of course, that this doesn't rise to the level of rape or kidnapping. Nonetheless, we should acknowledge that lying and capitalizing on a person's trust violate a person's autonomy just the same. It seems likely that a rational person would no more consent to being lied to and used in this fashion than she would consent to being a victim of date rape. This, at least, seems to be the implication of Kant's view and it reminds us that mutual respect is necessary in the everyday aspects of our lives.

Some may argue that Kant's deontological moral theory is too stringent in that it allows for no exceptions to the moral rules we discover. Shouldn't we make exceptions when doing so would make the world a better place? But maybe this is to miss the whole point. How much better a place could the world be than if everyone were obeying the Kantian perfect duties—not murdering, not stealing, keeping promises, etc.—and determining how best to fulfill the imperfect duties, doing all they can to develop their own talents and to help others in need? As ideal as Kant's notion of the "kingdom of ends" may sound, it leaves out certain salient aspects of the moral life. It excludes any reference to the development of human emotions and the role they play in our being able to respond sensitively to the moral demands of particular circumstances; it denies any moral value to actual happiness; and it conceives of duty as completely independent of and in no way constituted by a characteristically human desire to be and to do good.

ENDNOTES

1. Immanuel Kant, *The Foundations of the Metaphysics of Morals*. References here are to *The Foundations of the Metaphysics of Morals* translated by Lewis White Beck with Critical Essays Edited by Robert Paul Wolff (Bobbs-Merrill, 1982). In the first section of this work, Kant argues that morality is founded on a rational will, the only thing that is good without qualification. The good will is the source of our sense of moral duty.

2. Kant, p. 12.

3. See Kant, *The Foundations of the Metaphysics of Morals*. This section is a summary of ideas contained in section two of that work. There Kant argues that moral rules command unconditionally and derive from a supreme moral principle he calls the "categorical imperative." This principle is derived from rationality itself and not the particular characteristics of human nature—desires, inclinations, tendencies, etc. It would apply to any rational being. Kant distinguishes the categorical imperative from hypothetical imperatives that lay out conditions necessary to reach certain specified goals; the latter are not moral commands. Kant also gives several formulations of the categorical imperative, two of which—the principle of universalizability and the principle of respect for persons—are discussed here.

4. Note that for Kant the term 'person' does not mean the same thing as 'human being.' Any rational, autonomous being qualifies as a person. 'Human being' is a term that refers to our nature as determined by natural, empirical conditions. A human being is a natural thing; a person is not a thing but a value in and of itself.

STUDY QUESTIONS

1. What is *deontology*?
2. Describe the different kinds of deontological theories.
3. Explain Kant's concept of the good will. Consider the concepts of rationality, free will/autonomy, and duty as the moral motive. Is the good will the only thing that is good? Why does Kant say that good will is the only thing that is good *in itself*?
4. What is the difference between *hypothetical* and *categorical imperatives*?
5. What is a maxim?
6. Describe the *principle of universalizability* and the *principle of respect for persons*.
7. How is the categorical imperative used as a test procedure for determining moral duty?
8. Explain the difference between *perfect* and *imperfect duties*.
9. How does Kant distinguish between persons and things?

QUESTIONS FOR REFLECTION

1. For Kant, lying is always wrong no matter what the circumstances. What do you think? Can you imagine any circumstances when it might be morally permissible to lie? Give an example.
2. According to Kant, actions done out of inclination and without the intention to act on duty have no moral worth, even if they conform to duty. Do you think this is right? Do intentions matter that much?
3. Kant argues that because persons have value in themselves, we have a moral duty to treat persons with respect. Animals aren't persons. Does that mean we should treat animals as mere things, as Kant's theory implies? Do we have any moral obligations toward animals? What might a utilitarian say?

SUGGESTIONS FOR FURTHER READING

Aune, Bruce. *Kant's Theory of Morals*. Princeton: Princeton University Press, 1979.

Darwall, Stephen L., ed. *Deontology*. Oxford: Basil Blackwell, 2002.

Donagan, Alan. *The Theory of Morality*. Chicago: University of Chicago Press, 1977.

Korsgaard, Christine M. *Creating the Kingdom of Ends*. Cambridge: Cambridge University Press, 1996.

Langton, Rae. "Duty and Desolation." *Philosophy* 67, 1992.

O'Neill, Onora. *Acting on Principle*. New York: Columbia University Press, 1975.

Paton, H. J. *The Categorical Imperative*. Pennsylvania: University of Pennsylvania, 1947.

Schneewind, J. B. *Essays on the History of Moral Philosophy*. Oxford: Oxford University Press, 2010.

chapter 6

Virtue

Is the moral life taken up exclusively, or even primarily, with trying to determine which actions are right or wrong? From the perspective of normative ethical theories like utilitarianism and deontology, it would seem to be the case that we meet the demands of morality simply by adopting and applying the criteria for moral correctness. For utilitarianism, we only need to perform actions that bring about the best overall outcomes in order for those actions to qualify as morally good ones. Under that view, morality is solely a matter of improving the circumstances in the world, making it a better place by producing good consequences for the greatest number; intentions just don't matter. Kant's duty ethics provides a supreme moral principle—the categorical imperative—the application of which tests whether the rules we follow in acting can be universalized, whether an action counts as a duty. Under this view, the intention to perform an action because it is a duty is what exclusively determines the moral value of the action; consequences don't matter.

Because utilitarianism is concerned with overall happiness, it places no value on any one individual's happiness. Kantianism, too, places no value on an individual's happiness, not because it is overridden by a sense of the general welfare or because the individual cancels out, but because happiness is not the point of morality at all. There's a dilemma that emerges when we consider these two views in juxtaposition. On the one hand, there is a broad and sweeping notion of happiness without any recognition of the value of one's own personal qualities and ends. On the other hand, there is a large, looming notion of the moral agent, the individual, completely devoid of desires, natural inclinations, tendencies, and traits. When put in these terms, we may wonder whether either perspective could possibly portray morality as we live it in everyday life.

One reason the dilemma emerges at all is that both sides ignore something that seems so naturally a part of the moral life—a person's character. Character is understood not in some abstract sense as a general interest in producing a better world or as rational intention, but rather as a full measure of a person's reasons, desires, emotions, and dispositions—how they are organized in oneself and how they relate to a person's action. This is the focus of virtue ethics. Whereas consequentialist and deontological ethical theories are primarily concerned with identifying universal moral principles and determining how and when actions are morally right or wrong, virtue ethics is concerned more fundamentally with the development of a virtuous character. "What is the good life?" and "What kind of person should one be?" are the central questions of virtue ethics.

Virtue ethics, like consequentialism and deontology, is a normative ethical theory; in this regard it purports to be action-guiding. Unlike those theories, however, virtue ethics does not endeavor to identify a general moral principle like the utilitarian greatest happiness principle or the Kantian principle of universalizability; instead it seeks to understand what good character is and how that character informs our actions. Moral action cannot be understood in isolation from the kind of person one is, so the task of virtue ethics is to identify those traits of character that are exemplified in the virtuous person. So when we are considering what to do in a particular circumstance, we should ask: "What would the virtuous person do in this case?" We can think of this question in more specific terms when we consider particular virtues like courage or generosity. So we might ask "what would the courageous person do?" or "what would the generous person do?" Such questions are more complicated than they may initially appear to be in that they require we know what the virtues are, what it means to possess those virtues, and how it is that they lead to certain actions.

It is evident in ordinary life that not everyone is virtuous in exactly the same way. Virtue ethics, then, has to account for the wide variability of ways in which people can exhibit moral goodness. At the same time, it provides a context for understanding what virtue is, in general, and for understanding the purpose of leading a virtuous life at all. These are central points in Aristotle's conception of virtue as contained in his *Nichomachean Ethics,* the main focus of this chapter.[1]

Aristotle's Idea of Happiness

We can think of normative ethical theory from two moral perspectives: The perspective of action and the perspective of character. Aristotle's emphasis is on the question of character. His fundamental concern is to show how the cultivation of the virtues in us conduces to a flourishing, happy life. In order to do this, Aristotle views ethical theory in the larger context of a conception of human nature, one that seeks to identify the proper function and purpose of being human. According to Aristotle, everything aims at some goal, has some purpose. Natural things have this purpose built-in and function in such a way so as to realize their ends. In order to lead a moral life, we need to understand what that purpose is for us and to determine the best means for achieving it.

Aristotle's theory is a prime example of *teleology* (from the Greek *telos,* meaning purpose). A teleological conception of nature says that everything has a good at which it aims and in order to achieve that good, it exercises a function that is proper to the kind of thing it is. The goal of human nature, according to Aristotle, is happiness, where this is understood not simply as a particular conscious state or feeling, but as general well-being or the quality of a flourishing life. Happiness, in this sense, is lifelong pursuit accomplished by exercising the proper function of being human. Aristotle arrives at a notion of what constitutes our proper function by considering how we understand other kinds of things. For instance: Artists, musicians, and carpenters have functions; the various parts of the body—the eye, the heart, the kidneys, the lungs—each have a function. Wouldn't it be odd to assume that all these things have a function, but a human being does not? The function of a human being should be something particular to human beings. It cannot be just life, because all other living things have that. It cannot be sensation, because that is shared by animals. What distinguishes human beings from other living things is the capacity to reason, and it is in terms of the use of reason that we are directed toward happiness as a goal.

According to Aristotle, happiness is our greatest good, that which we desire for its own sake, and we desire all other goods in order to ultimately attain happiness. But what is happiness? Aristotle considers some common conceptions, or misconceptions, like happiness is pleasure, or honor, or wealth. The goal of anything is necessarily related to its proper function; if the proper function of being human is to be rational, then happiness is possible only for a being capable of reason. It should be evident then why Aristotle rejects the idea that happiness is the same thing as pleasure. Pleasure is not unique to humans. Animals with a high level of sentience are capable of feeling pleasure. Moreover, pleasure is a momentary sensation. It is there only as long as one experiences the feeling. Happiness is not just a momentary sensation or even a collection of good feelings, but rather "an activity of the soul"—as Aristotle calls it—in accordance with our rational capacity to develop the virtues. Happiness is not honor. Honor depends on what others think of us, and while it matters how others view us, this would be too superficial a notion of happiness. We pursue honor and wish to be viewed positively by others in order to reassure ourselves that we are good in some sense. So honor is not pursued for its own sake. For the same reason, wealth is not happiness, since we pursue wealth for the sake of something else.

In suggesting that happiness is "an activity of the soul" Aristotle doesn't mean to say that other goods, like pleasure, or honor, or wealth, aren't of value at all. On the contrary, he includes them in his analysis of a flourishing life precisely because it is hard to imagine how one can be happy if one suffers pain, has a bad reputation, and live in poverty. In this way his notion of happiness combines the teleological concept of proper function with the common sense idea that the material conditions of one's life make it difficult to attain happiness. At the same time, he believes that the virtuous person is best able to deal with adversity and the contingencies of life.

Happiness also consists in balancing reason and emotion. The emotions are not just unbridled desires that need to be reined in or suppressed by reason. Instead they can be imbued with rationality in the sense that we can develop an understanding of when and to what extent we should exhibit and act on our emotions. The moral life is lived not in isolation but with others, and the point of ethics is to enable us to live well with others. Our relationships with others in a moral community are wide and varied and involve the entire range of human capacities, not simply an intellectual awareness of what is right and wrong.

As with anything, human beings can function well or poorly. Happiness, in so far as it is an activity of our fundamental nature, is what it means for us to function well. It is the development, possession, and exercise of the virtues that constitutes the essential core of happiness. Only the virtuous person, the person with a firm and fixed good character, can attain happiness. The virtues, then, benefit those who have them and account for why the virtuous person can be said, in some sense, to have attained fulfillment even in the face of adversity and just plain bad luck. It is the vicious person that is truly miserable.

When Aristotle says that we are rational by nature he means that the power to reason is our distinctive function, but it is important to note that rationality is not simply a disposition that directs us toward knowledge and theoretical understanding. From the moral perspective, rationality is fundamentally an activity that, when exercised well, also leads us to frame the virtues for ourselves. The practical function of reason is to get us to live well in the world. Certainly this involves a kind of knowledge and under-standing, an exercise of what Aristotle calls the "intellectual vir-tues," but living well in the world involves more than just knowing things. It also involves acting and feeling, and these too can be done well or poorly. The achievement of a well-functioning life is accomplished through what Aristotle calls "practical wisdom" (*phronesis*). Think of it this way: To live well in the world, we don't just require an abstract understanding of what is right and wrong. We need to know what to do and how to direct our actions in particular situations—what to do when, what feelings to have and to what extent, what people are affected by our actions, and so on. So practical wisdom is an organizing activity, a special ability that aims at striking the right balance in action and feeling.

Aristotle's Theory of Virtue

What are the virtues specifically and how is it that we have them at all? In the first instance, Aristotle says that the virtues are not in us by nature; we need to acquire them. We do have a natu-ral capacity to acquire the virtues; that is the function of reason, but character is formed over time. The virtues are formed in us through habit. That is, we learn to be virtuous by practicing those actions that virtuous persons perform. This is the reason Aristotle claims that the virtues are not in us by nature: What is natural cannot be changed through habit. Natural capacities are innate and not acquired through habituation. We can come to be virtu-ous, to develop traits that go to constitute character. If the virtues were already in us by nature, there would be neither a need nor a way to acquire or change them. The idea of habituation is impor-tant here because it indicates that the virtues cannot be taught or learned in a purely intellectual way. Think analogously of learning to play a musical instrument; you can read all you want about it, but the only way to learn to play the guitar, for instance, is through practice. It is likewise with virtues such as courage or generosity. We can only come to be courageous or generous by persistently practicing courageous or generous acts.

Just as the virtues are formed through habit, so are the vices. If the virtues are formed through good habits, then the vices are formed through bad habits. You play the guitar, perhaps, but play it badly. Maybe you've developed bad habits with respect to certain mechanics, holding the instrument wrong, or fingering chords improperly; or maybe you fail in listening sufficiently to intonation and frequently play out of tune, etc. If these become ingrained, you will continue to play the guitar badly. It could change, of course, in that you might become a better guitar player, but not mystically or magically. You'd have to undo the bad habits (something which could be exceedingly difficult) and develop good ones. Here again it is likewise with the vices. If a person persistently acts in miserly or stingy ways and gets in the habit of doing so, then he or she will become a stingy person. To do so is to act less than reasonably or in accordance with our best nature. As a result one forms a bad character. To act in accordance with our rational nature, to practice good ways of behaving, will lead to the cultivation of a good character.

There is nonetheless an important difference between performing actions that we might call virtuous and actually being virtuous. Aristotle addresses this issue by first considering a puzzle about virtue, one that initially appears as a paradox. How can we become good, if we are not already good? Consider these two propositions:

1. To be virtuous, a person must perform virtuous acts.
2. In order to perform virtuous acts, one must already be virtuous.

If performing generous actions, for instance, requires that a person have a generous character, then that seems to violate the idea that we develop character only through practice and habit. But if a person develops a generous character only by acting generously, then that seems to violate the idea that only a generous person can act generously. This seems to imply that a person can be generous before he or she has developed a generous character. But that's precisely what Aristotle denies is possible, since virtues are not in us by nature but are learned through habit.

Aristotle's way of solving this puzzle is ingenious. He says that actions may conform to virtue but not yet be virtuous. Think of it adverbially: In order for an action to be virtuous it must be performed virtuously. That is, actions are virtuous when they are performed in the manner in which a virtuous person performs them. Most generally, this means that actions are virtuous when they are performed reasonably, in accordance with our best rational nature; but this doesn't say much. What precisely is the manner in which virtuous persons perform their actions? Aristotle specifies the conditions of acting virtuously by noting certain characteristics of the virtuous person. These are:

1. The virtuous person *knows* that a particular action is virtuous and understands why it is the right thing to do in a particular circumstance.

2. The virtuous person *decides* to perform the action and freely chooses to do so. In this sense, the virtuous person is motivated by his character and intends to perform an action because of it is judged to coincide with virtue.

3. The virtuous person acts from a *firm and unchanging state* and on the basis of habit has cultivated a good character.

In examining these requirements for virtuous actions, we can see the integral connection between a person's character and what a person does. That is, we can see the specific ways in which one's actions accord with reason.

Notice also that we can see how an action conforms to virtue but does not yet count as virtuous. Consider what and how we teach our children. A mother says to her six-year-old son, "Share your toys with your sister." The little boy does what his mother says, but he doesn't *know* why his action is good and is *motivated* not by the characteristic of the act itself, but perhaps by the avoidance of punishment or the expectation of a reward. He is simply following Mom's orders and does not freely *decide* to do it, and certainly doesn't act from a *firm and unchanging state* as he is just beginning to learn good habits and does not yet have a fully developed character.

This example demonstrates not only how we come to learn the virtues but also how important it is to have proper guidance in life. Moral education is not like theoretical learning; it can't be gotten by studying or reading a manual. Learning to be virtuous depends on living in a social environment—a family say—where there are those who serve as moral exemplars for us. The example also highlights the fact that without such guidance and in the absence of those who serve as moral exemplars, a person is at a distinct liability in that it becomes exceedingly difficult to learn those habits of acting that lead to the development of good character. Matters are even worse when those who guide others are themselves persons of bad character.

The virtuous person, then, is one who exercises practical wisdom and who understands the connection between reason and virtue and who knows the right thing to do in what circumstances. But just what is a virtue? Aristotle says that a virtue is an intermediate or mean between two extremes, one of excess and one of deficiency. He writes:

> Both excessive and defective exercise destroys the strength, and similarly drink or food which is above or below a certain amount destroys the health, while that which is proportionate both produces and increases and preserves it. So too is it, then, in the case of temperance and courage and the other virtues. The man who runs away from everything in fear, and faces up to nothing, becomes a coward; the man who is absolutely fearless, and will walk into anything, becomes rash. It is the same with the man who gets enjoyment from all the pleasures, abstaining from none: he is immoderate; whereas he who avoids all pleasures, like a boor, is a man of no sensitivity[2]

In acting virtuously, we try to strike a proper balance; there should never be too much excess or too much deficiency when it comes to the virtues. It is the extremes that damage people. For instance, a person who eats too much or eats too little will not be healthy. Similarly for the "soul," a person who acts in an extreme manner will not be virtuous. A virtue then is a state of character that exemplifies a balance between some form of excessiveness, on the one hand, and some form of deficiency, on the other. So the courageous person for example, is one who is neither excessively fearful nor rash or foolhardy. Think of this in ordinary terms. It is likely that you have encountered individuals who are incapable of dealing with even the most minimal kind of adversity; they seem to be paralyzed by fear. Then there are those who take unnecessary and foolish risks, who put themselves and others in jeopardy by doing so. Or perhaps you know a person with virtually no sense of humor at all, one who takes even the lightest of situations as an occasion for the deepest of reflections or a person who shows up at a serious occasion wearing a bulbous nose and slap shoes. Or maybe one of your friends is a sheer pleasure seeker and another seemingly devoid of any capacity to enjoy herself. You might have been embarrassed by a relative's extravagance in giving gifts or appalled by someone's stinginess. The story is the same in each case: Somewhere between the extremes is a properly balanced action.

This proper balance is what is sometimes called the "golden mean." The virtuous person effects this mean by doing the right thing, at the right time, and with the right aim. This applies not only straightforwardly to actions, but also to emotions, which have profound bearing on our relationships with others. Consider anger as an example. There are many occasions when we get angry without any real justification. Aristotle says it's easy to just get angry, anyone can do that. It is difficult, however, to manifest anger in a properly balanced (virtuous) way. It is difficult to be angry with the right person, to the right extent, at the right time, in the right way, with the right aim. This calls attention to just how hard it is to be virtuous and why developing a virtuous character is such a fine accomplishment. He writes:

> . . . it is no easy task to be good. For in everything it is no easy task to find the middle, e.g. to find the middle of a circle is not for everyone but for him who knows; so, too, any one can get angry—that is easy—or give or spend money; but to do this to the right person, to the right extent, at the right time, with the right motive, and in the right way, that is not for everyone, nor is it easy; wherefore goodness is both rare and laudable and noble.[3]

Aristotle recognizes that the notion that a virtue is a mean between extremes needs further clarification. There are three factors to consider in this regard. First, it should be understood that not every action or emotion has a mean. There can be no golden mean of actions like adultery. Consider an adulterer who attempts to justify his actions by saying he didn't commit too much adultery or too little, but given the circumstances just the right amount. He committed adultery with the right person, to the right extent, at the right time, in the right way, with the right aim. That would be preposterous. This is also the case with certain emotions, which by their nature are destructive. Take envy for instance—envy is the feeling of being pained by the good fortune of others. Is there ever a properly balanced way to express that emotion in a moral context? Some actions and emotions are wrong because they are already extremes, already deficiencies and so could not conduce to one's happiness and, in fact, are destructive to those who perform such actions or cultivate such emotions. No extreme could ever qualify as a virtuous character.

Second, Aristotle says the mean is "relative to us." There is no one position that is the intermediate for every person; the mean is not the same for everyone. For some people going into a burning building would be reckless, for others it would be appropriate and courageous. If one has asthma and is frail, then it would be foolish to attempt a daring rescue in a burning building; but for a trained firefighter with appropriate strength and skill it would be a courageous act. We wouldn't think that the asthmatic is a coward for not running into the burning building, though we might think that a firefighter that refused to do is weak in virtue. Likewise while we think it would be reckless for the asthmatic to run into the burning building, we wouldn't think that the firefighter is reckless for doing so. The mean is the appropriate way of acting given our individual strengths and weaknesses and the particular circumstances in which we are called upon to act. Recklessness and cowardice are both vices in that they are extremes that involve, in this case, too little or too much fear. No extreme can be measured in a rational way. In this sense, no extreme can ever count as a virtue. This is another way of understanding why it is difficult to fix on the mean. There is no formula for doing so. Instead we need to employ a wealth of knowledge in making a determination of how to act. We need to know our own states of character, our particular strengths and weaknesses, and our own inclinations. We need to know who will be affected by our actions and what the circumstances are. This requires that we put our reason to use and exercise the practical wisdom required to function well. It may be that certain states of character are so firmly fixed in us that they become "second nature," but even with this it is impossible to predict all that life might throw our way. Practical wisdom and a well-developed character are the best means available to deal with whatever contingencies may arise.

Third, following from the idea that the mean is "relative to us" and in the absence of a general formula for determining an exact mean that applies to all persons in all circumstances, Aristotle proposes three general guiding principles that, when applied, give us the best chance of hitting the mean. These are:

1. Avoid that extreme that is more opposed to the mean.
2. Avoid the easier extreme.
3. Be careful with pleasure.

One extreme is more opposed to the other. Let's stick with courage as an example. Courage is more like rash behavior in that it requires a diminished sense of fear. In this regard, cowardice is the extreme more opposed to the mean. So we should avoid being overly fearful. Generosity is closer to extravagance than to miserliness, so avoid being stingy. But we also need to take account of individual tendencies, and so some person might find it easier to be rash and reckless. In that case, the easier extreme should be avoided. Pleasure poses a particularly difficult problem for us. There is nothing wrong in feeling pleasure, in fact we become insensitive if we try to avoid it altogether. A little reflection demonstrates, however, that the difficulty emerges because it is initially seems so natural to feel pleasure at the extremes. So the macho man feels pleasure in his daredevil behavior, the coward in knowing that he wasn't at any risk, the glutton in overeating, the cigarette smoker in her nicotine fix, and the promiscuous person in self-indulgent, profligate sex. To such individuals, even the mean seems painful. But if practical reason can lead to a moderation of behavior and the development of habits that cultivate better states of character, then we could conceivably learn to take pleasure in being virtuous.

Some Final Thoughts

There are several criticisms of virtue theory that bring us back to many of the issues examined throughout this text. A common argument against virtue ethics is that it is insufficiently normative or action-guiding; it does not provide a set of rules for determining what actions are right or wrong. At least, utilitarianism and Kantian deontology give criteria for deciding what actions are right or wrong. The virtue theorist might respond that action is guided not so much by rules or principles as it is guided by character, and since there is no one way to be a person of good character, different actions may be required of different individuals. The fundamental point of ethics is to aid, then, in the cultivation of those states that lead to good actions.

In a related way, some criticize virtue theory because it relies too heavily on the contingencies of human life and the notion of moral luck. Other normative theories try, at least, to minimize the role of luck (utilitarianism) or eliminate it altogether (deontology). If we are to hold people responsible for their actions, to praise or blame them for their actions, then there must be a clear and objective basis on which to make such judgments. Virtue theory recognizes, however, that it is just a fact that the circumstances of life are beyond our control. Some people are lucky enough to have proper guidance and good moral exemplars that aid in the development of good character, while others are at a liability because they lack that guidance and are confronted with only bad influences. But such factors alone do not completely determine how one turns out. As Aristotle himself suggested, the virtues best equip us to deal with adversity. Developing the virtues and sustaining them is difficult under any circumstance; we are all vulnerable to life's contingencies and any goodness we achieve is itself fragile. This is an "essential feature of the human condition, which makes the attainment of the good life all the more valuable."[4]

Some say that virtue ethics is just a fancy form of egoism in that it focuses on oneself and emphasizes how one benefits from having the virtues. One who holds this view might argue further that if the goal is happiness, then all my actions are in some sense directed toward my ultimate interest. But this seems to miss the point about happiness. It's not that we act just so that we feel happy, but rather that our well-being depends on how well we exercise practical judgment in developing a character that enables us to live well with others. The virtues, then, are not just self-directed, in having them a person performs actions that necessarily benefit others. There is no contradiction in also saying that the virtues benefit those who possess them.

Others argue that virtue ethics implies relativism. Aristotle's own theory, they might suggest, is suitable for a Greek aristocrat, but some other culture may value other virtues. This too is to miss a salient feature of the idea of virtue. Namely that the goal of ethics is to lead a moral life in a community, to live well with others, and though there may be some variability in how that is accomplished, it can't be that we could function well in a moral community without any conception of virtues like justice, truthfulness, generosity, courage, and friendliness. Some virtues are requirements for any human being to lead a flourishing life. In addition, the relativist denies that there is an objective human nature. Virtue theory requires that a general human capacity, reason, if you will, be put to practical use in determining how best to live in the circumstances in which one finds oneself. The application of the virtues may indeed be "context-sensitive," but that there are virtues at all is not.[5]

Virtue theory may have an advantage over other normative ethical theories in so far as it recognizes that we cannot separate morality from the world as we find it, that we cannot act in isolation from those with whom we actually live, that we cannot exclude desires from our pursuit of moral goodness, and that we have not succeeded in living well by just following rules and doing good things. If character is source of action, then it matters what kind of persons we are.

ENDNOTES

1. This chapter provides a brief summary of some central ideas in Aristotle's *Nichomachean Ethics*. Specifically, it focuses on the idea of happiness, the theory that virtue is a "mean between extremes," and the idea of virtue as a state of character. There are numerous translations of this work; a particularly readable one is: *The Nichomachean Ethics*, translated by W. D. Ross (Oxford University Press, 1959). References here are to that translation.

2. Aristotle, *Nichomachean Ethics*, Book II, chapter 2.

3. Aristotle, *Nichomachean Ethics*, Book II, chapter 9.

4. See the entry on virtue ethics by Nafsika Athanassoulis in the Internet Encyclopedia of Philosophy (http://www.iep. utm.edu/virtue/).

5. See Martha C. Nussbaum, "Non-Relative Virtues: An Aristotelian Approach," in *The Quality of Life*, edited by Martha C. Nussbaum and Amartya Sen, (Oxford University Press, 1993) pp. 242–70.

STUDY QUESTIONS

1. How does virtue ethics differ from consequentialism and deontology?
2. What is *teleology*? In what sense is Aristotle's virtue ethics *teleological*?
3. Explain Aristotle's conception of happiness. How is happiness different from pleasure?
4. What is the fundamental difference between "intellectual virtues" and "moral virtues"? What is "practical wisdom"?
5. Aristotle argues that the virtues are not in us by nature. How so? How, according to Aristotle, do we acquire the virtues?
6. What puzzle about virtue does Aristotle present? What is his solution?
7. What does it mean to say that "an action is virtuous when it is performed virtuously"? What is the manner in which a virtuous person acts?
8. Explain the idea that virtue is a mean between extremes. What is the "golden mean"? Aristotle says that the mean is "relative to us." Explain that idea and think of some examples of your own.
9. Though there is no exact way to hit the mean, Aristotle provides several general guidelines. What are they?

QUESTIONS FOR REFLECTION

1. Is morality primarily about performing right actions or being good persons?
2. Do you think it is difficult to be virtuous?
3. How might the virtues benefit those who possess them? What has character got to do with happiness?
4. Aristotle's conception of the virtues is grounded in the idea that human beings have an essential function. Do you think we have such a function? Is happiness our purpose?

SUGGESTIONS FOR FURTHER READING

Anscombe, G. E. M. "Modern Moral Philosophy," *Philosophy*: 33, 1958.

Bennett, Jonathan. "The Conscience of Huckleberry Finn," *Philosophy*: 49, 1974.

Foot, Philippa. *Virtues and Vices*. Oxford: Blackwell, 1978.

Hursthouse, Rosalind. *On Virtue Ethics*. Oxford: Oxford University Press, 1999.

MacIntyre, Alasdair. *After Virtue*. London: Duckworth, 1985.

Mayo, Bernard. *Ethics and the Moral Life*. New York: St. Martin's Press, 1958.

Murdoch, Iris. *The Sovereignty of Good*. London: Ark, 1985.

Nussbaum, Martha C. "Virtue Ethics: A Misleading Category?" *Journal of Ethics*: 3, 1999.

Shklar, Judith N. *Ordinary Vices*. Cambridge, MA: Harvard University Press, 1984.

Taylor, Gabriele. *Deadly Vices*. Oxford: Oxford University Press, 2006.

About the Author

Alex Eodice is Professor of Philosophy and Chair of the Philosophy Department at Iona College, where he has also served as Director of Honors and, from 2001–2008, as Dean of the School of Arts and Science. He holds a PhD in philosophy from Fordham University and a professional certificate in Management and Leadership in Education (MLE) from the Harvard Institutes for Higher Education. In  2009, he was named a visiting scholar at Blackfriars Hall, Oxford University where he conducted research and delivered a lecture on legal obligation and coercion. His publications include articles on the concept of moral innocence, the nature of law, and the philosophies of Wittgenstein, Dewey, and St. Augustine. In addition to his academic pursuits, he enjoys golf, collects vintage guitars, and plays in a local blues band. From 1992–1999, he was an elected member of the City Council in New Rochelle, NY, where he currently resides with his family.